William C. Dunlap

Life of S. Miller Willis, the Fire Baptized Lay Evangelist

A man who literally took God at His Word for twenty-six years, and yet never wanted for any good thing

William C. Dunlap

Life of S. Miller Willis, the Fire Baptized Lay Evangelist
A man who literally took God at His Word for twenty-six years, and yet never wanted for any good thing

ISBN/EAN: 9783337251437

Printed in Europe, USA, Canada, Australia, Japan

Cover: Foto ©Lupo / pixelio.de

More available books at **www.hansebooks.com**

S. MILLER WILLIS.

LIFE

OF

S. MILLER WILLIS,

The Fire Baptized Lay Evangelist.

A MAN WHO LITERALLY TOOK GOD AT HIS WORD FOR TWENTY-SIX YEARS, AND YET NEVER WANTED FOR ANY GOOD THING.

BY

REV. W. C. DUNLAP

ATLANTA, GA.:
CONSTITUTION PUBLISHING COMPANY.
1892.

Entered according to Act of Congress, in the year 1892,
BY THE CONSTITUTION PUBLISHING COMPANY,
in the Office of the Librarian of Congress, at Washington.

INDEX.

	PAGE.
Frontispiece—Likeness of Miller Willis	1
Title page	3
Dedication	5
Preface	6
Introduction, by Rev. W. A. Dodge	7–8

CHAPTER I.

His Parents—Birthplace—Early Childhood, Youth, and Going to Sea 9–18

CHAPTER II.

His Life of Wickedness Continues—Becoming Worse and Worse Until it Almost Eventuates in a Horrible Murder 19–25

CHAPTER III.

His Experience in the Army, Including His Conversion in 1864, and the Life He Lived, and the Work He Did in the Church and Sunday-school 26–32

CHAPTER IV.

Miller Willis as a Member and Worker in the Church and Sunday-school Continued, from His Joining in 1864 to 1877, Including Some Thrilling Experiences in Pushing the Work of Soul-saving. 33–43

CHAPTER V.

His First Visit to Thomson Circuit, North Georgia Conference, and What Resulted to Himself, and the Good Through Him that Came to Others 44-55

CHAPTER VI.

In Charleston, S. C. His First Experience in Open Air Meetings, together with Many Other Exciting Scenes and Narrow Escapes with His Life, which He Passed Through in Prosecuting His Work 55-64

CHAPTER VII.

A Continuation of His Work, Including Experiences that Remind the Reader of the Heroic Days of Methodism—A Policeman Waiting at the Door of the Church to take Him to Jail...................... 65-72

CHAPTER VIII.

His Visit to the —— Circuit, North Georgia Conference, and the Work of God in that Charge while He was There—Taken from His Memorandum Book........ 73-81

CHAPTER IX.

With Rev. E. B. Rees on Fairmont Circuit, North Georgia Conference—An Account of the Wonderful Work of Grace on that Charge as Related by Himself, Together with an Article Written by Rev. W. A. Parks, and Published in the *Wesleyan Christian Advocate* 82-88

CHAPTER X.

Miller Willis and the Holiness Movement.. 89-93

CHAPTER XI.

Miller Willis as a Bible Student   94-108

CHAPTER XII.

A Short Chapter Giving a Few Samples of Miller's Letters, Together with Some Answers from Correspondents 109-119

CHAPTER XIII.

Miller Willis' Scrap Book 120-165

CHAPTER XIV.

Millis Willis, by Rev. R. W. Bigham, of North Georgia Conference 166-176

CHAPTER XV.

Miller Willis, by Rev. R. W. Bigham, Continued 177-190

CHAPTER XVI.

Impression of Miller Willis, by Rev. C. C. Carey, of the North Georgia Conference, M. E. Church, South...191-198

CHAPTER XVII.

Miller Willis, (from Rev. M. D. Smith, of North Georgia Conference)... 199-206

CHAPTER XVIII.

Letter from Rev. T. B. Reynolds, of the Florida Conference, M. E. Church, South. 207-211

CHAPTER XIX.

Letters from R. K. Moseley, Seward, Ga.; Rev. James L. Ivey, Rutledge, Ga., and Dr. H. V. Hardwick, of Conyers, Ga..212–221

CHAPTER XX.

Letter to the Editor from Brother Sam Hunter, of Athens, Ga..222–233

CHAPTER XXI.

From Robt. A. Adam, His Brother-in-law...............234–251

CHAPTER XXII.

Funeral Service in Honor of Brother Miller Willis at St. James Church, Augusta, Ga., July 16, 4 o'clock P. M..252–268

CHAPTER XXIII.

Articles from Various Newspapers, Christian and Secular, on the Life and Death of Miller Willis.........268–276

CHAPTER XXIV.

Miller Willis Articles Copied from Newspapers Continued...277–286

CHAPTER XXV.

His Last Days 287–293

PREFACE.

The compilation and editorial work involved in the preparation of the Life of MILLER WILLIS has been performed under the peculiar disadvantages of an itinerant ministry. When first commenced the Editor was in a city pastorate with seven hundred members. Then came a move of two hundred and seventy miles, into a Presiding Eldership of eighteen charges, embracing nearly ten counties in Northwest Georgia. The work was undertaken for the Glory of God, and in response to what seemed the practically unanimous call from my brethren. I need hardly say that love for our dear Miller has been a strong incentive from the beginning. The work makes no pretensions to any literary merit. The Editor has striven, at any cost to mere style or grammatical construction, to present a true life picture of our glorified friend. With the hope that it may help to carry forward the great work of spreading Scriptural Holiness, to which Miller Willis, while living, gave all his ransomed powers, it is hereby given to the public.

DEDICATION.

To the Lord Jesus Christ, first:—and to all those Living and in Glory, second; whose experience and lives stand for the great doctrine of Apostolic Christianity—Entire Sanctification—and for the Defense and Perpetuity of which Methodism was, Providentially, under John and Charles Wesley, raised up:—this book is reverently dedicated.

INTRODUCTION.

In sending forth this volume to the public, we are aware, that on the line of biography it is hard to find anything new. But in this instance we have the life of a man peculiar under grace to himself. He takes his place along by the side of the immortal Carvosso, Billy Bray, and other men of like character. And as the lives of such men are read and blessed to the good of thousands, we believe that this volume will be read and re-read by thousands living and yet unborn to profit.

We have known of him from our boyhood, and in later years much about him from personal observation and experience, but from the beginning we have been impressed with the fact of his likeness to no other man living or dead, that we have seen or of whom we have read. He was God's chosen vessel, and a channel through whom He could work and speak without let or hindrance. His motto was, "Obey God, rather than man." Naturally brave, and, when fully sanctified, he became God's hero to do things that no one else would think of or dare to do. By some he was thought to be cranky, but it was that peculiarity that comes from a man, by grace, becoming so much unlike the world and so much like Christ, that he did not talk and act like the world about him. Where he was known best he was loved most. While he was as bold as a lion for God and the truth, he was never known to lift his voice in his own defense. He left all that with Him to whom he belonged. "When reviled, he reviled not again." With a nature made by grace as gentle as a woman and as brave as a lion, he was ready for any work that opened up to him.

The reader will be impressed most of all, with his simple child-like faith in every word of sacred truth. He accepted every command and promise without questioning. "Have faith in God," was his watchword. We have heard his voice ring out clarion-like many times with this text from the lips of his divine Lord. His last utterance on earth was: "Trusting Jesus now and forever, Amen." We pray that the reading of this book may be sanctified to the good of all.

W. A. DODGE.

LIFE OF S. MILLER WILLIS.

The Fire Baptized Lay Evangelist.

CHAPTER I.

His Parents—Birthplace—Early Childhood—Youth—and Going to Sea.

S. MILLER WILLIS was the son of A. G. Willis, who died in 1852. His mother was Mrs. Sophronia I. Willis, daughter of Dr. J. L. E. W. Sheecut. They were both born in Charleston, South Carolina.

His father was for many years connected with the *Augusta Constitutionalist*. His brothers were Edward, Hermon B., Milton H. and James G. He had but one sister, Sophronia I., the wife of Mr. Robert M. Adam. Of these, only Major Edward Willis, of Charleston, and Mrs. Adam, of Spartanburg, S. C., are now living.

Miller was born in Hamburg, S. C., Jan. 29th, 1839, and departed this life July 15th, 1891—being fifty-two years, six months and six days old at the time of his death.

His parents moved across the Savannah River, into Augusta, Ga., when he was an infant. This city he always claimed and spoke of as his home. Here his father and mother died and are buried. Here he was brought up, except as he rambled off for a time. He was converted here, and his remains were brought here, and his funeral preached, and in her beautiful cemetery his body rests, awaiting the ressurrection of the just.

In old St. James, of Augusta, he always kept his membership, except for a short while—a year or two—he was a member of Trinity church, Charleston. He joined the church under the ministry of Rev. James E. Evans, of blessed memory—"Uncle Jimmy," as he delighted to call him.

His father dying, left Miller with only his mother to guide and control him. He was naturally self-willed and impetuous in his disposition. He was of small build, low of stature, and of a frail appearance. He was the most active boy in school—almost a perfect athlete. He enjoyed the advantages of an ordinary education.

After this brief statement, I come to a somewhat lengthy account of his youthful days, as given by himself. I confess to some little hesitancy to giving in detail, just as he writes it down, all the wickedness he charges against himself; but as I wish to preserve the true character of the man, I give it in his own language. He left this record of his badness, I know, only that he might magnify the grace of God, that saved such a wretched sinner as he was. No man ever prayed more, or labored harder, to get little children converted and to keep them from going into sin, than he did. This was his standing scripture for children: "My little children, these things write I unto you, that ye sin not." I. John, ii: 1." We make these references to head off any possible license that might be taken by the young that, because Miller Willis was saved, and became such a holy man, after being so wicked in his youthful days, therefore, they can postpone their return to God later in life.

According to his brother, Maj. Ed. Willis, it was in 1856, that he conceived the idea that he must go to sea. His mother, of course, was opposed to it. But so reckless and determined was he, that he told his mother that if she would not give her consent, he would run away.

But before giving the narrative with the adventures of going to sea, he tells three incidents, illustrative of his daring disposition, as also of the wonderful Providence that saved him from an untimely and violent death.

The first was, in riding a wild horse, standing with his feet on the horse's back, and driving him at a breakneck speed over a bridge, the horse fell, pitching Miller headlong to the ground and breaking his arm in three places. From this frightful hurt he was weeks recovering; but he was hardly well before he came very near losing his life, by falling out of a tree forty feet high. He was picked up senseless, and apparently dead. But he seemed to be preserved only that he might find death in a watery grave; for, being out on the Savannah River in a boat one cold winter day all alone, with a thick winter suit on, he fell backwards in the middle of the river. Here was made available his wonderful powers as a swimmer, which his brother Ed. speaks of in writing of him to me. After relating these fearful adventures and escapes from death, he makes this entry: "The Lord spared me, though I was so wicked and disobedient; yet He preserved my life, and, oh! the promises I made to Him, and soon forgot them."

His going to sea was an epoch in his early life—not for good, surely, judging from the evil influences he was brought under; and yet, there seems to be, in some inexplicable way, an ever present over-watching Providence that attended the wreckless boy, and that ever and anon brought him under the real fear of death and hell. Say what you please about fear as an incentive to religion, one thing is certain, so far as Miller Willis is concerned, it was one of the most powerful breaks on his downward train to perdition. Indeed, one is almost forced to the conclusion, as one reads his own account of himself, that but for this element in his nature he would have leaped head-long into hell before he was fifteen years old. Afraid of man? He seems to have been an absolute stranger to any such emotion. One other influence ought to stand in the fore-front as a check upon him, and which he always associated with those other influences that held him back in his downward career—the love of his mother. How to reconcile his life of sin and disobedience to every precept of maternal love, I do not undertake to explain, but now and again, right in the very act of grieving and almost breaking her heart, he breaks out, "Oh, how

I did love my dear mother," or "I do know I love my mother." But to the story of his sea-faring, etc.

"Now, my father was gone, and I was left with a widowed mother in Augusta, and oh! how I loved my mother. I told her I was going to sea. I said I will run away and go if you don't let me go. So my dear mother said: 'Rather than you should run away, I will write your brother Ed and let him get you a place.' My brother was in the employ of John Fraser & Co., Charleston, S. C. So he said: 'Wait awhile and you can go.' They were building a new ship—'The Eliza Bonsall' was her name, and this was her first trip. We left from Charleston, 1852, in the summer. Sister Wightman [the bishop's mother, I take it.—ED.] gave me a Bible, and put in it these words: 'If sinners entice thee, consent thou not.' Ever remember 'Thou God seest me,' and then her name." He makes this confession: "I never opened that Bible while at sea." But he says, "I prayed and cried to God to save me, and made great promises to God. I went to the captain's wife and said, while all was getting dark in the day, 'What is the matter with the pigs?' for we had two of them aboard, and I thought the wind was the pigs squealing. The captain's wife told me it was the wind. I was scared then, for I thought surely the ship can't stand that wind against her, and the waves rolled over her time and again. It was getting black now, for the night was on us. Oh, how I did go among some old sails and pray for God to spare me to get back home to my dear mother. But soon the wind ceased, and then I forgot what I had promised in the middle of the Atlantic ocean. A man aboard the ship—an 'Elliott street runner'—from Liverpool, England, told me one night he must have some tobacco, and heard I had a lot of it. I told him he could not get mine. As I was a great tobacco user myself, I did not intend to allow them to get my tobacco, and I had heard it was gold in Liverpool. I had several pounds, and could get what I wanted for it when I got there. This man—'Liverpool Johnnie'—was the 'runner's' name, and I got into a dispute about the tobacco, when he threatened to throw me overboard. I had a large sheaf knife, and I told him I would drive it through him if he came in my room without first knocking at my door; for I was afraid he would throw me overboard, for I slept in about three feet of the rail in the midshipman's locker, and he was a dreadful man. My tobacco was in charge of the captain, and no sailor dared to go in his cabin without permission, so I felt it was safe. When we got to Liverpool we found a guard standing at the dock gate, who examined every one who passed out to see that he had nothing that duty was to be paid on. A man goes out with a plug of tobacco tied around his neck and one around his body, and in this way many plugs went out without duty being paid on them.

I was walking the streets of Liverpool one day and met a man with a lot of miser's purses; they were little strong pieces of cloth sewed up so you could not find the opening to them without understanding how to work them. The man seemed very humble until I had bought a lot of little things from him, among them the miser's purse. I said, the purse is no account to me, for I cannot open it; then he began to assert himself. 'Oh,' says he, 'you give me a penny and I will show you how to open it.' I saw in a moment the trap I was in, and handing him the penny, he gave me the secret. I was then without religion, and something to fill the void was what I wanted. I found out the truth of this scripture —Isa. lvii, 20-21. I wanted peace and could not find it. I went in that great city of ships and flags, and I found out—'The wicked are like the troubled sea, when it cannot rest, whose waters cast up mire and dirt. There is no peace, sayeth my God, to the wicked.' I was out at night in this wicked city, and oh, what I saw was enough to ruin any poor boy like myself. I went with 'Liverpool Johnnie' one night into a dance house; in front was a bar room, and in the back was a place filled with round tables, with men and women seated around them. When I entered the room, they cried out, 'Come here, my Yankee lad.' Beautiful young women, all playing for beer, and laughing so loud that the *kind* and *tender-hearted* barkeeper would have to quiet them now and again. It was all new to me, and to be made so much of by all, turned my head; I thought I was somebody. But all of a sudden a great fear came over me, and I cried, 'here, take me right out of here, and let me go quick, or I will tell the captain all about you.' I did not have sense enough to see that at any moment one of those men or women could seize me and get 'advance' money for me, by getting me aboard some ship going out of Liverpool. But God took care of me even then. As God was with Joseph, so He was with me even then, and I knew it not. Think of bad women by the dozen, parading the streets decoying men. One took hold of me one night, a beautiful little Scotch girl, with black eyes, and said, 'you are my cousin so and so.' 'Oh no,' I said, 'I don't know who you are talking about.' 'Well then, stand for my beer, wont you?' 'No, no,' I answered, for I was astounded at such things. But oh, I was getting into the trap and I did not know it. The captain said it was dangerous for me to go out on the dock after night, and said he would take me up to London with him, and that I must not go out at night any more. Little did he know the places I had been in, with desperate men, too.

The two pigs we had aboard were named 'Dennis' and 'Patrick.' They would catch a rat and shake him to pieces and then eat him. We would take a beet or a piece of cabbage and bait the traps, and the rats would fill the traps so full that they would kill each other. When the ship would be in a calm we would take a lump of coal and put cotton all around it, and then throw it into the sea, and I could see it, it seemed to me, nearly three-quarters of an hour, going down, down into the depths of the ocean; and just so, Oh Lord, I feel thy poor unworthy child ought to go down, down, for Thou hast said, 'For every one that exalteth himself shalt be abased, and he that humbleth himself shall be exalted.' Luke xviii: 14.

We were out forty-four days and nights on the ocean; no land, nothing but birds for our company, and all sorts of fish. I saw several whales spout the water up, and I saw sharks.

When we got off the coast of Ireland, men and boys came in fishing smacks to trade fish for old clothes. I gave some of my old clothes for pity's sake. On our way over, one day at sea, the cabin boy and I got into a dispute. I touched him lightly on the face, when he drew out a sheath-knife and drove it into my hip. I took a brick he was cleaning his knives and forks with, and nearly knocked his brains out. The captain was going to whip him. I said, 'No, I can take care of myself.' The boy begged me not to have him taken up when I got back to Charleston. I told him I would not think of such a thing.

So I got back home, and was lost. I was a wicked, wild fellow, and no stirring scenes to engage me. Oh, how I longed for something wild to see or read. It was nothing else except this that made me go to sea, and now nothing but my mother's love kept me home, and would not let me go back. But I began to read wild books, such as "Claud Duval," "Jack Shephard," "Sixteen String Jack," and many more of the same kind. We had a band there we called "The Seven Brothers of Augusta," and if being wicked made us brothers, then we were certainly blood-kin. We met in our hay-loft, and oh! at such times, we would plot mischief—get hold of things, fair or unfair—and then we would all get together and divide and eat and make plans for getting hold of more; then we would sell and divide.

I want to say just here, for the glory of God, that one other and I are the only two on our way to heaven, out of all my companions; and many, or nearly all, are dead; or gone, some in Texas, some in places I don't know where. But hallelujah to God! I am on my way to heaven. Oh, how often I think, suppose I had had religion then, what a blessing God could have made me to them. One of my best friends came home during one of my stays at home during the war. I heard by chance they had brought the dear boy home, but oh how sad to say it—he was in his coffin. Though a wicked boy, when I went in and heard it was the dear fellow-boy, the friend of my youth, my heart smote me. I was soon to go back to the army again, and I was not sure but that I might be brought back in my coffin, too, and oh how sad it made me to think I had not obeyed the Lord. Mathew vi: 33—"Seek ye first the kingdom of God, and His righteousness, and all these things shall be added unto you."

CHAPTER II.

His Life of Wickedness Continues—Becoming Worse and Worse, until it Almost Eventuates in a Horrible Murder.

With his return from sea he seems to have plunged headlong into sin, with a recklessness that betokened a soul truly lost to all moral and religious restraint; but not so. His conscience, at times, would suddenly start up with all the fury of outraged law, and lash him into a perfect frenzy of prayer and promises. These times of seeming penitence came usually in connection with some desperate act—may be next to murder. But let us follow him in his own words, as he exposes his vile conduct without a single paliating circumstance. Like the Holy Scriptures, in their dealings with the best men of the Bible, they do not seek to cover up or modify any bad conduct, so Miller Willis uncovers himself as the embodiment of meanness.

Slapping the Men in the Face, in 1855 and 1856, at the South Carolina R. R.

"The trains used to stop at the S. C. depot in those days—men getting on the train. We [I suppose he means " The Seven Brothers"—Ed.] would go up to the windows and talk with them. The platform was not far from the river railroad bridge—so when the train would start off, we would either slap the man in his face, or we would spit in his face. We would chew our tobacco and get a mouthful of the juice and spit in their faces, and then run off. They would come to the platform of the car and swear vengeance against us, saying they were a great mind to jump off the train and catch us, and that they knew our faces, and they would certainly prosecute us and make us pay for daring to slap so and so in the face. But on the thing would go in a few days after the same way.

"At one time I went up to the window and began a conversation with a powerful man—large and strong—and when the train started off I spit tobacco juice in his eyes, then slapped his face and ran off. He threw a large knife and struck me. I picked it up and ran off with it. They would not jump off, though they would make great threats to do so. Thus we continued to go on getting worse and worse. We would go into each bar-room and look for men that were drunk, and on the street, and if we found them we would take them up stairs in the old market house, where there was a pair of stocks and fasten their hands and feet, and one —— ——, being a strong young man, would lay on about 39 lashes. Oh, how they would curse and swear—how they were going to make us pay for it when they got down stairs. But we would make them promise to go home and say nothing to any one as they went. One or two would follow them across to Carolina, and then leave them. If they came back the band would be scattered." Of course this sort of conduct, with much else he relates of himself and his wicked associates, could only have been carried on with any sort of impunity at night. Besides, he says: "There were only two policemen in Augusta at that time, and they were old men, and so we had just as good a time as if there were none." I will stop here to say what does not appear in his account of himself. At this time, according to the testimony of his brother, he was hard at work during the day. But God could and did speak to him even through his wickedness. Hear him: "I never can forget the last time I ever troubled a drunken man, and the impression it made on me for good." He found a man drunk on the street, and, somehow, in his playing pranks on him, he thought he had broken the fellow's neck, and he ran off and cried and prayed to God, making all sorts of promises; if the Lord would not let the man die he would never trouble another drunk man. And this time he kept that promise. But now comes one of the most fearful adventures of his life: "On one occasion I went to the race track, and on that day came near driving my own precious mother mad, or causing her death. She said often if they brought me home dead, well and good; but if they brought me home a murderer she would die sure. It would either kill her or she would lose her mind; and I did love my precious mother. I would promise never to touch any one again to harm them, but soon I was into something worse. While on the race track, I whooped and yelled like a demon, until a race rider got mad because I was yelling for the mare that won the race, and in a rage he came to me and said: 'Now, you hush, or I will slap you down.' 'Well,' I said, 'you are big enough, but if you do I will be with you when you do it.' So he slapped me down, and as I rose I stuck my knife in him three or four times. The blood flew all over me and him. In a moment I was gone, and they were hunting the person that stabbed him.

'Where is the man that killed him?' everybody was exclaiming, 'for a man like him can't live.' Oh, how I felt. 'Now I am a murderer, I have killed a man and my mother too.' So I went for home, and when I got there my mother cried, 'Oh, my son, you are at last a murderer; oh, you have killed your mother! Some boys coming from the race track told me you had killed that race rider.'

Oh, how I prayed, and promised God if He would spare the race rider, and my mother, I would never be guilty of such another act. If the Lord ever helped a wicked boy to pray more than He did me, I never heard of him. I thought surely, never, while I have breath, will I ever do this again; and then I would say to myself, will you let a man slap you down and not resent it? No, never, I will kill any man that slaps me down, and I will be thought well of by my friends for doing it. [Here is the public sentiment that has made many murderers.—Ed.] My wicked heart had murder in it, and my friends said I was right. But oh, like the prodigal son in Luke xv: 13, I was 'wasting my substance in riotous living, and no man gave unto me,' except bad advice. They were my companions that said unto me, 'go on,' and we thought other people did not have the fun we had, so on we went."

THE EXPLOSION.

"We lived next door to an old lady, Miss ———, [I omit the name,—Ed.] and oh, how precise and prim she was; the least noise would start her off, and oh, how she would talk of it all day long. A lot of us boys got a piece of blasting fuse—they blasted rock with it— some called it safety fuse. The hydrant we used water out of was between the two families; on either side of the fence there was a tub filled with water, and we got a small glass vial and filled it with powder, then put the fuse in and stopped the vial well to keep the powder dry. When all was ready we lighted the fuse and walked off leisurely down the street as if nothing was the matter. The fuse being long gave us ample time to get a good distance before the powder caught. In eight or ten minutes the explosion came, and away went the tub, water and all, against the house. Miss ——— thought it was one of us and she was going to see that we were taken up for it, and made to go before the mayor. My precious mother was in the house, and when Miss ——— charged her boy with it, she was hurt, and went over to Miss ———'s. 'Oh,' says Miss ———, 'they might have blown the house up; I will send for the owner of the house and I will make them see sights yet, yes I will,' and off she sent for the owner of the house. 'See here, see here! just look where it threw the staves. If some one had been passing along the street they might have been killed.' 'My children were away down town when it happened," said my mother. 'Don't care if they were four miles away, they did it, and I know it,' said Miss ———. My mother was troubled and hurt, for we told her we did not do it. How could we when we were away down town when it occurred. Our precious mother believed her children, just as, I guess, most mothers will. No one but us knew how it was done either."

As he looked back many years afterwards, and recalled those wayward acts of his young life—as if speaking from the time these things took place, he utters this prayer, and this appeal to those who might be ready to cast the first stone.

"I would say, Lord, do spare me awhile longer, and let me see Thy mercy. Lxxxvi Psalm and 5th verse: 'For Thou Lord, art good, and ready to forgive; and plenteous in mercy unto all them that call upon Thee.' And because God was good and ready to forgive, therefore I went on deeper and deeper in sin, and forgot God and Heaven. Reader, how is it with thee? Have you never promised to do better, and then done worse than before?"

The following is the last mention he makes of his wicked life, except the account he gives of himself during the war. He gives no date, but it must have been some time after he had become religious. "I was walking down Broad street, Augusta, and met Mr. ———— near the old D'Antiagnae building; he stopped me and said: 'You see Miller Willis so sober? Ah! that fellow has done devilment enough to damn him.' But I could praise God and say, if it had not been for the mercy of God I would have been a lost soul to-day; but bless God, He saves me—even *me now*. Hallelujah to Jesus!'"

CHAPTER III.

His Experience in the Army—Including His Conversion in 1864, and the Life He Lived and the Work He Did in the Church and Sunday-School.

We come now to one of the most intensely interesting chapters in Miller's life. Of the war, as such, he says but little. His mind is too full of other and greater things. Whatever may have been his feeling at the breaking out of the war, and no doubt they were intense, when he came to write of himself in connection with those times, he was a new man—God had taken all sectional bitterness and hatred out of his heart. While he was still a Southern man, yet he loved his Christian brethren of the North, and ascribed his experience, especially in Holiness, largely to the writings of Christian men and women North. The "Guide to Holiness" was one of the first periodicals that woke up his heart to the glorious truth that there was a deeper and more satisfactory experience in grace than that which was obtained in conversion.

But we shall say no more here about this; further on in another chapter it will be seen more at large how much he loved, and how gladly he acknowledged his indebtedness to these brethren. He enlisted in the army in 1862, and, up to the time of his first discharge was in the Army of Northern Virginia. How many battles he was in he does not say, but he was wounded twice in both knees. I presume, though he does not say so, that this was the cause of his being discharged. After his discharge from the Virginia army, he was in an artillery company on the coast. This incident is given me by Major Willis, his brother, and it sounds just like Miller Willis:

General Drayton, of South Carolina, going into a fight found Miller, gun in hand, away behind the company, and said to him, "Why are you not with your command?" Miller answered, "Don't you see I am afoot? You are on horseback; why don't you go to the front? Go ahead, and I'll be there as soon as wanted. I am ready to follow—you just lead the way." But to resume his own narrative: "We were in a piece of woods, when the enemy got our range and began to kill us by the dozen. A young fellow in a few feet of me was killed, and several wounded. I cried out: 'Boys, boys! you may like this, but I would rather be at home eating milk and peaches.' All near me laughed out right there in the presence of death, so hardened had we become in our hearts. But next day came the fearful second battle of Manassas. While on the march I saw a young man at the foot of the hill at Brandy Station, Va., his feet bare and nearly in the little stream. I looked at him, and wept for the first time in years. I thought, just as that young man is, so it will be with me soon. My mother will get the news that I am killed and lying out here barefooted like him. But I soon forgot, and was as wicked as ever. I think it was about 3 or 4 in the evening we were marched to the scene of battle—second Manassas—horses, wild and riderless, loose on the plains, men praying, swearing, throwing away their cards, and pressing their Bibles next to their hearts. Now men made great promises, as the wounded and bleeding ones were being brought out. I nearly fainted with fright. I trembled from head to foot, and made a thousand promises. I vowed and re-vowed if the Lord would only spare me to see my dear mother one more time how I would serve Him. But Satan told me, 'Yes, you have said that many times before, and you did not do it. You told a lie to the Lord. Yes, and so often have you promised you don't believe yourself.' Try me, Lord, one more time, and then if I do not be a good boy, kill me. The shells were flying, and men crying and swearing, and some praying, for I was one of them. Sure I had never prayed like that before. While lying on my face, with my gun by my side, a shell tore it to atoms, and a piece struck me on my knee. Oh, how I prayed, and promised the Lord I would do as He bid me from that moment to the end of my life. There I was, helpless before God, and far from home, about to die among strangers. I thought I was dead. After awhile along came some boys from Augusta. 'Well, here is Miller Willis!' They saw my gun shattered to pieces. 'Are you wounded?' they asked me. 'I am a dead man.'

'Where are you wounded?' One of them took me by the hand and lifted me up. 'Old fellow, I don't see the blood.' I examined, when I came to myself, and saw it was only a small red place where I was wounded. They said: 'You are not hurt.' I could not believe it, for oh, I was so frightened that I could not realize that it was my own feet I was standing on. But each moment I was making some new vow or promise to God. Soon after this we were on a forced march to Gordonsville, then to Staunton and Winchester. Not long after we got there I was examined by the surgeon and discharged, my discharge being signed by General Lee. But it soon got so no paper would do any good. I then volunteered and went to the coast of South Carolina. I was here, I believe, six months in an artillery company—Giradeau's battery." This must have been after his conversion, for he says: "I left Augusta still not what I felt I ought to be. My carnality troubled me, and I sought sanctification, 1st Thes. v. and 23, October 6th, 1877, and received it to the joy of my soul—entire sanctification—after living a converted life like Mathew xviii and 3, from 1864 until 6th October, 1877."

According to his own account, as written to Rev. George G. N. McDonald, his conversion was attributable to a sermon he preached in St. John's church, Augusta, Ga. Brother M. was preaching, as Miller thought, from the text, "Pay thy vows." Though Brother M. says his text was another passage, so that the explanation must be, Miller either did not notice the text, or else it had been announced before he came in, and the first word he heard as he entered was, "Pay thy vows!" he very naturally thought that was the text. The preacher went on to say, "You have made many vows on the battlefield that if the Lord would spare you to get home to your dear mother, you would be a Christian." He heard nothing else, for he was shot through and through by the arrow of divine truth. Although he had in a measure been brought up under Episcopal influence, yet, he always preferred the Methodist; and of Methodist churches, he always preferred to have his membership at St. James, and I think we might say of preachers, up to that time, he preferred Rev. J. E. Evans, D.D. But it was some little time after his awakening and joining the church before he was consciously pardoned. Often have I heard him relate it. His agony of soul reached a state of such suffering that he felt if deliverance did not come, and come speedily, he should die. It was while in this state of mind that one night on Ellis street, about ten o'clock, he felt he must have religion or perish. So with this conviction upon him he resolved to go into the barn, the place where he and his wicked associates, with the devil, had often conferred together how to carry on his work. But now that he was about to break with him and his work forever, what better or more fit place than in that same barn. He seems to have been on the street when this purpose was formed in his heart, for he says: "As I threw the gate open that led into the barnyard, down came the Lord Jesus into my soul!" and he began to shout, "I've got it! I've got it!" So overwhelmed was he with this new joy, that he felt he could not wait until morning before he told it, and so he began to knock up the neighbors to tell them the good news; for most of them were gone to bed. "What's the matter?" they said. "Oh! I've got religion! I've got religion!" But alas! alas! he began to realize now what he never had cared for before—that the neighbors did not believe him. They said: "Oh! it's Miller Willis at some more of his devilment, and this time he's making sport of religion." But when they came to know that he really had professed religion, they said: "Oh! well, it won't last. He'll be back in his wickedness in a few weeks." Oh, how many souls have been discouraged, if not really driven back into sin, by such evil prophesies as this, and frequently by members of the church. But, thank God, their predictions never came true about Miller Willis. His was a "sky blue conversion," as he delighted to call it, quoting after Bishop George F. Pierce, "and I knew it, just as well as I know my right arm from my left, and I know it now, twenty-three years afterwards. Praise the Lord."

But here is the letter which he wrote to Brother MacDonell, acknowledging him as his spiritual father:

Brother George MacDonell, M. E. Preacher, Thomasville, Ga.:
 DEAR BROTHER:—Twenty-five years ago you passed through Augusta. I was just out of the army of Northern Virginia. And oh! how at the second battle of Manassas I promised God if He would only spare me, what a boy I would be for Him. I was spared wonderfully. While trying in part to fulfil my promise to God, I walked in there, and you, a stran-

ger in Augusta and to me, and to all as far as I could hear, preached at St. Johns M. E. church. Your text was, "Pay thy vows." Your first remark was: "There are young men in the house who promised God upon many battle-fields, 'only spare me and I will serve you any way you lead me.'" I said to the young man next to me, "Did you tell that preacher that?" "No," said he, "I never saw the preacher before." "Well then, God must have told him, for I have told no living person."

I went next day to Uncle James E. Evans, and told him all. I joined St. James M. E. Church, and went to work for the Lord. Since then I have been in Trion, N. C., Charleston, S. C., and from Augusta, Ga., to Fairmount, in North Georgia, and in nearly every town and city, from here to there, and talked Jesus to them.

I felt I could delay no longer to write you, that God used you to awake me from sleep and death. Am now in Milledgeville, Ga., and expect, D. V., to go to Florida.

May God bless you and yours, and help you to stir many more, and save their souls. He that hath said: "Call unto me and I will answer thee, and will show thee great and mighty things which thou knowest not," (Jer. xxxiii: 3) will help you, I pray. Mark xi: 24.

Yours, less than the least. 1 Thessalonians, v: 23.

S. MILLER WILLIS.

Now with Bro. J. R. King, Milledgeville, Ga.
Feb. 18, 1889.

Miller Willis joined the church before he was converted. Here is a lesson for those who do not believe in joining the church until after they are converted. Maybe if he had not done so he would have backslid from the mighty conviction of the Spirit. No doubt Uncle "Jimmie" Evans advised him to go right straight and join the church. Thank God, he did it.

CHAPTER IV.

MILLER WILLIS AS A MEMBER AND WORKER IN THE CHURCH AND SUNDAY-SCHOOL, FROM HIS JOINING IN 1864 TO 1877, INCLUDING SOME THRILLING EXPERIENCES IN PUSHING THE WORK OF SOUL-SAVING.

While he has not left so full an account of his life and work during this period of his life, yet there will be found many striking incidents interspersed along in other parts of these pages—some with dates, and some without dates, that must have transpired between 1864 and 1877.

Besides, there is ample oral testimony that he was an indefatigable worker, both in prayer-meetings, class-meetings, and Sunday-schools; but especially, was he everywhere to be found in the sick room, administering both to soul and body. He did a vast deal of this sort of work. He was peculiarly adapted to it. He became so well known, and was so successful in administering consolation, and even in leading penitent sinners, on their death bed, to faith in Jesus, that he was often sent for instead of the regular pastor. Men who made no open profession of religion had a standing arrangement with their friends, that when they came to their last sickness, if it were possible to get Miller Willis, they wanted him sent for in preference to priest or preacher, that he might pray for them, and administer the consolations of religion to them. A striking example of this sort occurred in Augusta, Ga., last year, (1891.) A man, who, in his early years had been under Catholic influence, when he grew up and came in contact with Protestant truth and light, practically broke away from its ignorance and superstition, yet did not profess experimental Christianity, but had it understood with the lady with whom he boarded, and who had been a mother to him, that if Miller Willis were accessible when he came to die, she must send for him. This lady was herself a member of St. James church. Strange enough, while Miller was in Augusta attending the Interstate Holiness meeting, and with the writer some time after, helping in a meeting at Asbury church, this man was stricken down with what proved to be his last illness. Miller was sent for, and day after day he visited and prayed for the sick man. There is good reason to hope he led him to a saving knowledge of the Lord Jesus Christ, though a great outrage was committed by the Roman Catholics both before and after the man's death. They took advantage of the fact, that the lady at whose house he was sick was a widow, and the further fact, that she herself was sick and confined to her room up stairs, to bring a priest just before he died, who tried to force "extreme unction" with the last sacrament on him, but the dying man actually clasped his teeth together and refused, though they tried to put the wafer between his teeth. After his death, they took forcible possession of his body, carried him to the

Catholic church, and buried him with Romish rites. Speaking of this, reminds me: Miller and the Romanists could never harmonize. The Romanists, and especially the Romish women, who are employed to do work that their men can't do, used to hate Miller with a perfect hatred; and, I am almost afraid he thought he was doing God's service to hate them, especially before he was sanctified. More then than even now, they tried to furnish all the hospital nurses, and even to exclude all Protestant visitation and service from the sick. Miller had no idea of being ruled out from this field of labor, and so he and they used to have some serious conflicts, they even threatening to have him pitched out at the window, while he would defy and dare them to attempt it. He become so aroused on the Roman Catholic question once that he sent off and procured a large supply of tracts and other literature and scattered them broadcast over the city. While his mind underwent no change, so far as the corruption in general of that church is concerned, yet, he greatly modified his methods of opposition to them. After reading the lives of Madam Guyan, Thomas A. Kempis, and Fenelon, he come to believe that even a member of the Roman Catholic church could get religion and be saved.

Sometime in the early part of his religious life he had an experience on the question of obedience that he never forgot. He was impressed that he ought to speak to people, whenever he met them, about their souls, but he shrank from it—he knew of no one else who did it—

not even among the preachers; he felt an apprehension of what it would cost him; he refused for a time to obey this unusual leading of the Divine Spirit; the consequence was he went into a state of spiritual darkness, of a most indescribable nature. He compares it to being taken up by the heels and put headforemost into a barrel of tar.

"TAR BARREL, AND HOW I WENT IN HEADFOREMOST AND GOT OUT OF IT."

"I was lead to talk to several who gave me a cursing, but I remembered what I promised the Lord when I was down headforemost in a barrel of tar. I felt as if some one had taken me by the heels and dropped me headforemost into a barrel of tar—could describe the darkness with nothing else, it seemed to me; then I told the Lord, 'I will do what You say, and at all times now and forever; just take me up out of here and I will serve You—yes, as I never saw any one else do—I will do it, Jesus!' He heard my cry and I was happy and joyous again. Oh, how I did delight to do Thy will, O my Lord! Yea, Thy law is within my heart." Ps. xi and 8.

THE SAD DEATH OF A YOUNG MAN—BOY YOU MIGHT SAY—ONLY 16 YEARS OLD, WHO WAS CALLED TO PREACH.

"In 1868 Rev. Geo. H. Pattillo was pastor of St. James Church, Augusta, Ga.

"A young man sent for me one night in a hurry.

He had come back from Oxford, Ga. He told me he was called to preach. 'Oh, Brother ———,' I said, 'don't resist God!' 'You know, Brother Willis, a boy sixteen years old can't preach.' 'Yes he can if God calls him to it.' He cried, he prayed, but told me, 'I can't preach.' I begged him not to resist God. He said he wanted to preach, but how could he without an education.

"Soon the dear boy was taken ill. I went to see him. Brother Pattillo was there; I think he called on each one of us to pray. Brother ——— was delirious; he said, while his mind was wandering, 'I am climbing up a steep embankment, and now I am in the mud; Oh, how it hurt me to fall that time, but I am up again, and now I will get to the top.' Then he would cry out, 'Oh, I am safe now, and on the top.' Then he would talk and get happy, and soon he was so weak, but he said, 'I have committed the sin unto death; I will go to heaven, but if the Lord would spare me I would preach, young as I am.' 'If any man see his brother sin a sin which is not unto death, he shall ask, and he shall give him life for them that sin not unto death: There is a sin unto death. I do not say that he shall pray for it.' 1 John, 5 ch., 16 verse. Brother ——— knew he had to die—he knew he had committed the 'sin unto death,' and he gave no reason to hope he would get well. When spoken to about getting well, he would say: 'Yes, young as I am, I would do my best to preach,' and in the next breath he would tell how he wanted to be buried, and what songs he wanted them to sing over his grave—showing he did not expect to get well. 'Sing,' he would say, 'Rest for the weary,' 'Sweet rest in Heaven,'

> 'Come, schoolmates, don't grow weary,
>   But let us journey on;
>   The moments will not tarry,
>   This life will soon be gone.'

"And so our young men's prayer-meeting was peopling Heaven. Oh! bless God for the young men's prayer-meeting at St. James church, Augusta, Ga. It landed many in Heaven, and was the life of the church.

"So died our dear Brother ———. Farewell, Brother ———, by the grace of God I'll meet you."

Bless the Lord, he kept that promise, and no doubt he and his dear young brother are together in Heaven.

Speaking of young men—how intense was the love of Miller Willis for this class of souls. He knew their temptations and danger, and oh, how he longed to rescue them from their perils by bringing them to Jesus. But his religion was of the most intense order; he could not long tolerate or coöperate, much less fellowship, any other sort. Hence, while he tried hard to fall into line with the Y. M. C. A. in their work, yet he and they found that two could not walk together except they be agreed—Miller was too red-hot for them, and they were too icy cold and formalistic for him. I have often heard him say that he never essayed to enter a pulpit but once. He was appointed to lead a Y. M. C. A. meeting, and some one persuaded him to go into the pulpit. He said it was the biggest failure of his life, and he said then if he could be forgiven for trying to act the preacher that time, he'd never do so any more. He always said the floor was his place. "I am nothing but a little five-cent fellow—like a nickle with a hole in it." He was often called "Reverend" by those who did not know him, but he never asked for, or desired license to preach. Here is his testimony to the love he bears for young men: "Oh! that I could speak to young men, and they could see the love I have for them, so they might take my advice and prepare to meet their God *now*, while the Lord calls to them saying, 'except ye be converted and become as little children, ye shall not enter into the kingdom of Heaven.'" Math. xviii: 3d verse. "So we see that no man can go to Heaven without being converted. Won't you turn *now*, dear reader, before the harvest is past and the summer is ended, and I am not saved? But, bless God, that is not my experience, but I am saved up to this moment, amen! And oh! if like the dear boy that was dying in the hospital, and cried 'here! here!' and when the nurses came and laid him upon his pillow and said: 'Did you want us when you shouted 'here! here?' 'Oh, no! I heard the roll-call in Heaven, and was answering to my name.' Oh! brethren, I can answer to mine, praise the Lord. Oh! can you say, 'here am I, Lord—send me anywhere on earth, at any time!' I know I am ready for Heaven while on earth; like Colossians, 1st chap. and 12th verse, 'Made meet to be partakers of the saints in light.' 'But who hath believed our report, and to whom is the arm of the Lord revealed?' Isa. liii and 1. Oh! that salvation were as common as any other business of life. You remember John iii, 14, 15, 16: 'And as Moses lifted up the serpent in the wilderness, even so must the son of man be lifted up, that whosoever believeth on him should not perish, but have eternal life.' 'For God so loved the world that He gave His only begotten Son that whosoever believeth in Him should not perish, but have everlasting life.' So the serpent is raised upon a pole, and the mother comes to her son, who is bitten, and says: 'Look, son, at that brazen serpent on that pole!' 'For what, mother?' 'To cure you.' See, here is a young man who has been bitten, and he is cured. 'How did he get cured?' asks the young man in the tent door, for the mother has pulled him out so he can look at the serpent. 'Look out, now, my son, at the serpent.' 'No, no! mother; if you will boil some herbs, and give them to me, or put a plaster on the bite, then you may say there is some reason in it; but just to look at a brass serpent—what virtue is there in that?' and so the dear young man dies, and there is no help for it.' 'But without faith it is impossible to please Him.' Hebrews xi and 6th verse. Now, brethren, we see God can't be pleased with us without faith—but what sort of faith? Not the faith that does nothing, but the working kind, or that which obeys God. 1 Saml., xv and 22. And Samuel said: 'Hath the Lord as great delight in burnt offerings and sacrifices, as obeying the voice of the Lord? Behold, to obey is better than sacrifice, and to hearken than the fat of rams.'"

HIS FIRST WORK OUT OF AUGUSTA.

About the years 1875 and 1876, he began to extend his work outside of Augusta—especially in the counties of Richmond, Columbia, and other counties then embraced in the Augusta district. Rev. R. W. Bigham was on the District, and Rev. B. F. Farris, now in Heaven, was pastor, first on the Richmond, then on the Appling circuit.

Through the instrumentalities of these brethren, Brother Willis began to work abroad. He describes his first call from Augusta to work in Columbia county, and the results under God:

"Miss ———, of Columbia county, would tell me of a church that was there when she was a small girl, but long since had been burned down. Oh! how it fired my young heart, and I resolved if ever I could, I would like to go to that deserted neighborhood. But I had no money and knew no one there; yet I cried to the Lord to open the way. One day I was told the preacher would be glad for me to come and help him, and I got a letter telling me so. Oh! I could have shouted and praised the Lord all day and night for a new place to work. I got with the preacher, and found a church floored with rough edge boards, and a few brothers and sisters there singing with all their might. Soon the work began, and one and another got Mathew 18 and 3, and some one or two got sanctified like First Thes, 5 and 23. Gamblers gave up gambling; sisters came and got the fear of death taken away by getting First Epistle of John, 4 and 17: 'Herein is our love made perfect, that we may have boldness in the day of Judgment, because as he is, so are we in this world.''

The preacher referred to was Rev. B. F. Farris, and I think it is St. Mary's church; if this is the church, it was here he had a singular experience in getting lost in the woods, and a remarkable answer to prayer in finding his way to the church. Among other strange characteristics of him, he took no knowledge of the points of the compass—the consequence was he got easily lost in a strange place. He took a walk out in the woods, and the first thing he knew he was completely turned round. He could not tell for the life of him where he was, or which way the church or the road was. Just as soon as he realized his condition, he fell down on his knees and began to cry to God for deliverance, when lo and behold, he had hardly opened his mouth in prayer, before they struck up a song at the church, not more than one hundred yards away. With a shout of joy he sprang to his feet and rushed to the place of worship. Seizing upon the circumstance of his being lost, he made a most powerful appeal to sinners to realize the awful fact that they were lost, and to run to Jesus like he had run from the woods to the house.

It made a wonderful impression, and some were saved by it. He was a true soldier—he knew the first lesson

—obedience. You could count on him doing what you told him. Capt. Farris was a true Gospel preacher. No quailing before men by him, or daubing with untempered mortar, or crying peace when there was no peace. They were true yoke fellows. The parsonage of the Appling circuit was located at a little railroad station. Just across the railroad diagonally a brother was running a barroom. Farris had shot him from the pulpit, so he became offended and stayed away from church. What was to be done? No thought of giving him up. So, after a counsel of war, Capt. Farris and his faithful lieutenant, Willis, decided that they would resort to sharp-shooting. Farris had been a brave captain in the war, Willis had been a soldier. They knew what that meant. Daily, for I don't know how long, until the enemy surrendered, Willis would go out on the railroad embankment and shoot red-hot messages out of Heaven's Artillery at the whisky-selling brother. What was the result? The brother gave up the bad business, came back to church and got saved, and for nearly twenty years he has been one of the pillars of the church and most spiritually minded man in all that part of the country. He'll meet Capt. Farris and Miller Willis in Heaven after awhile, and they'll have a good time talking over these things. Miller Willis' name is a household word in all that country to-day. Many will rise up in the resurrection morn and call him blessed.

CHAPTER V.

His First Visit to Thomson Circuit, North Georgia Conference, and What Resulted to Himself, and the Good Through Him that Came to Others.

His first visit to my charge, association with me in my work, and going with me from appointment to appointment, as well as pastoral visiting, were notable events, both to himself and many others. Just here I want to put on record my indebtedness to him for the example he set in this delicate, but all-important part of a pastor's work—pastoral visitation. While I would not adopt all his methods, yet I would say, be *filled* with the one purpose that dominated him—the salvation of souls—and methods will take care of themselves. He had a passion for souls. It could be said of him, as it was of his Master, "The zeal of thine house hath eaten me up." "This *one* thing I do," was a favorite quotation with him. He was what the world and worldly professors would call a "one idea" man.

It was during this visit, as told by himself, and recounted more than once in other parts of this book, that he obtained for the second time the experience of entire Sanctification; for, as stated by Rev. C. C. Cary, and as he told me when he first came to me in Thomson, he had surely entered into it only a short while before under the ministry of Rev. B. F. Farris, at the Richmond camp-meeting; and yet, Brother Farris had unwittingly talked him out of it only a few minutes after he had obtained it. He had become deeply concerned on the subject of holiness, first by reading "The Guide to Holiness," and then other papers and books—besides, Capt. Farris was an intense believer, and preacher of the doctrine, as taught in the Bible and the Methodist standards. Miller went, therefore, to the camp-meeting under conviction for a pure heart; the preaching, especially by Capt. Farris, intensified this conviction; he felt that he *must* have the blessing. At the close of a service—perhaps eleven o'clock on Sunday—he retired to the grove, as he expressed it, "to have it out with the Lord." While thus wrestling alone in prayer the baptism of perfect love came upon him. He immediately went back to the camp and told Brother Farris what he had experienced in the woods. Capt. Farris did not profess the experience, though he preached the doctrine, and defended the Paulian-Wesleyan view of it against all opposers. So far as I know he never did distinctively and avowedly profess the experience as long as he lived. Some years after this, I heard him (I mean Capt. Farris) almost testify to the blessing. This was at Gainesville, Georgia, during a holiness meeting. I have made this digression in speaking of Brother Farris for a purpose: he preached the doctrine, but he did not himself enter in by faith; the consequence was, while he was one of the best men among us in his life and morals, and very successful in getting sinners converted, he never led any one into the conscious assurance of entire sanctification, except in this one instance—and then he doubted its genuineness. And "the babe in Christ," just beginning to walk by faith, tottered and fell. There is a lesson for many of us just here. It is better to put the experience, or life, too high, than to put it too low; but it is much better to give the true Bible "standard," and encourage all to claim it on the Gospel terms—unconditional consecration, and simple faith in Jesus.

THE MEETING AT MT. OLIVET.

From this meeting, at White Oak Church, where he was wholly sanctified, we went to a little church called Mt. Olivet. It was rather an out-of-the-way place, some very good people living near, but not strong enough to keep up a regular church organization, and so the preachers gave them odd appointments, with sometimes a few days protracted meeting. This was an extraordinary time. God was present in soul-awakening and saving power. He gave wonderful liberty in preaching His word. I saw a whole congregation swept as by a cyclone of divine power. The hardest sinners surrendered or ran away. The results were largely due to the presence and labors of Miller Willis.

HIS GREAT FAITHFULNESS IN SPEAKING TO EVERY ONE ON THE SUBJECT OF RELIGION.

He was frequently with me from 1877 to 1884, sometimes spending weeks with me. It was during these most intimate associations that I came to know him in all the phases of his character and temperament. He never allowed an opportunity to escape to speak personally to every one he met. Sometimes I almost chided him for being over zealous at this point; but I was always restrained by the solemn conviction that he was specially called of God to this peculiar mission.

After faithfully warning a colored man, he would hold a class-meeting with himself after this sort: "Now, if that had been a white man—dressed fine, riding in a thousand dollar carriage and pulled by a thousand dollar span of horses, would I have dealt as plainly with him as I did with that colored man?"

This seemed to reverse the order of things, as practiced by some of us. We are more ready to give the gospel to the rich and great—*our* sort of gospel, at least—than we are to the mean and poor.

IN THE FAMILY.

He was a perfect gentleman everywhere and always. He was considerate of others, especially ladies; hence, he was as little trouble in the family as any one could be. He was as one of my family when with us. He was quick to observe any seeming neglect that involved any unnecessary hardship on my wife or daughters, and he would say to me: "Now, beloved, thus and so ought not to be."

WHY DID MILLER WILLIS NEVER MARRY?

Was it because of any disappointment in any love affair while a young man? No; not that I ever heard of; and I think he would have told me. Was it because he reached a point in Christian experience where he was not susceptible to the tender passion for the opposite sex? On the other hand I never knew any man more impressible than he was. True, it was only a select class with which he fell in love. But let him meet a pretty, religious, intelligent, and refined young lady, and then let her get wholly sanctified, and get up and tell it, and be *sweet* and *brave* enough to pray in public; and then look out for Miller's heart; he was in great danger of losing it in such a case. He told me of several love scrapes he had. The only difference between him and other lovers was he never would tell it to the young lady. He always told the Lord, and sometimes he would tell a sympathizing brother. He did not believe in, nor did he ever assume any priestly vow of celibacy; only he knew it was not for him to marry, if he would do the work God had called him to do; but he never hinted in the remotest sense that it would be a sin for him or any other Christian man to marry. He remained unmarried, I have no doubt, for the same reason that St. Paul did. He exhorted young people when they married alway to be sure it was in the Lord.

THE LOST BOOK, AND WHAT COME OF IT.

Perhaps there was no characteristic of Miller Willis as a Christian more striking than his unwavering trust in the overruling, ever present providence of God. He was the antipodes of a blind fatality, either on account of irrevocable decrees, growing out of the eternal sovereignty of God, or, what amounts to nearly the same thing, so perfectly carried away with eyeless optimism as to ignore personal responsibility for results. He was a Christian optimist, rather than an optimistic Christian. He used to say, "I never have any disappointments, because I let God make all my appointments." He committed himself *wholly* to God, and then trusted in Him. He did accept everything concerning himself as from God, but it was as a Christian he did it. He was neither an optimist or a pessimist in the modern popular meaning of those terms.

We give what in itself seems a trivial incident, but the sequel shows what a great result sometimes come from little things. He and I had been to the Richmond camp-meeting, near Augusta, and were returning to Thomson. As was our custom, we carried a good book to read along the way. This time it was a book written by Dr. Asa Mahan, called "The True Believer." It was the book, by the by, of all others, except the Bible, that convicted me of the need of entire sanctification by showing me that I had the seed of all sin in my heart—unbelief. We had read the book through going down. We lost it in the piny woods, traveling a neighborhood road, as we came back. I regretted the loss of it mainly at the time because it happened to be a copy I had given to my oldest daughter. But Brother Willis accepted it as of the Lord. I dismissed the fact from my mind. That was in 1877. In 1890 I was sent as the pastor to Asbury church, Augusta. One of the most devoutly religious families in the church was known by the name of Read. Soon after my arrival, I was invited round to the house of this family to a young people's meeting. Imagine, if you can, my surprise to find the lost book lying on his table. It had been largely instrumental in bringing the whole family into the experience of perfect love. He had found it soon after we dropped it, and had kept it in his family for thirteen years. My daughter's name was in the book, but during all these years he never had met any of my family until now.

"ON WITH THE LIME, PRESCOTT, ON WITH THE LIME!"

In the midst of great opposition to holiness, Brother Willis used to tell this incident to illustrate the necessity of pushing the doctrine on the Church: Years ago, Augusta had been visited with the yellow fever scourge. It was therefore of the greatest importance to have the city thoroughly policed, and disinfected with lime. But, like many about holiness, the people did not like for the Inspector to be prying 'round their premises, especially their back yards, so they gave him great trouble. He went to the Mayor several times, and told him how abusive the people were, until finally the Mayor could stand it no longer. He cut the matter short in this way: "Prescott! Prescott!! this city *must* be disinfected; don't come to me any more with the opposition of the people—right on with the lime, Prescott—right on with the lime!" Thus, he said, we must right on with holiness, and pay no attention to opposition.

THE SIN OF EVIL SPEAKING.

For this sin he had a special horror. He became aroused as to its frequency and enormity in the Church in this way: He had Mr. Wesley's sermon on the "Cure and Prevention of Evil Speaking" in tract form.

Our custom was, when we were out in the country, to go to the woods to read, meditate and pray. We read that sermon, and re-read it. Then we got down and read it on our knees, and by the time we got through with the third reading we were both thoroughly convicted that we were guilty of this most common sin. I was so full of the subject that I was obliged to preach on it, which I did a few days afterwards. At the close I called for penitents on that line, and Miller was the first to come; finally the whole church came. Brother Willis was prostrate on the floor crying for mercy for himself and the balance of us. I called on him to lead in the prayer. Never shall I forget that prayer. It took on a personal form in an unusual degree, and he prayed with awful vehemence. One petition I remember actually frightened me. It was, that "God may strike me (him) dead, rather than to let me (him) be guilty of the sin of evil speaking." I wish the whole church would read that sermon of Mr. Wesley's and get under conviction as Miller Willis did.

HIS RULE OF GIVING.

A great many people thought he was a religious pauper, going about living on the charity of the people. This was a great mistake. His brother in Charleston, S. C., Maj. Willis, or his brother-in-law, Mr. Robt. Adam, of Spartanburg, S. C., at whose house he died, Mr. Sam Hunter, of Athens, Ga., Josiah Miller, whose house was his home when in Augusta, Ga., and hundreds of others all over Georgia and South Carolina, were ready at any moment to supply his every want. But he literally obeyed his divine Lord, taking "no thought for the morrow," and yet he was seldom without money.

His rule of giving was one-half. If some one gave him $10.00, he set apart $5.00 of it as the Lord's—and he frequently gave the other five also. He paid his church dues regularly. Frequently he would not hear his pastor once a year preach, but he faithfully paid his quarterage.

THE TRIAL OF HIS FAITH.

This was frequent, and often sharp, and sometimes for quite a while; but as a rule it was simply a "fiery dart" from the adversary, and failing to make any impression, it was soon over.

When he first began to have hemorrhages—once I remember in particular—it was in Gainesville, Ga. He was up stairs, and was bleeding fearfully. He could not, for quite a time, make any one hear; it looked like his time had come. The enemy was there, and said: "Well, you have often said you were ready *now*, this *moment*, if God should call you to go. The moment has come; can you say it now?" Instantly his faith answered back: "Yes, glory to God! I'm ready."

"NOW, SAY AMEN."

"I was going from Augusta to Athens, and from Athens over to Macon, and from there to Fair Mount, in Gordon county, Georgia. After I had been on the train for some time, I missed my satchels, with all I had on earth in them. I had been at so many different places on my route, I could not for the life of me tell where I had left them. I would think one moment I had left them in Athens on the railroad platform, and then I would think no, I must have left them in Macon. I became perfectly confused in my mind. Something said to me: 'Say amen! you tell everybody else to say amen; now take your own medicine.' I said: 'Lord, every thing I have in the world is in those satchels—all my clothes and books; all I have been gathering for years;' and still something said: 'Say amen.' Then I said: 'I will; though he slay me, yet will I trust him.' I put my hand in my pocket-book; it felt heavy; I knew it was not filled with money. I opened it, and almost praised the Lord aloud, as I repeated 137th Psalm and 1st verse: 'I will bless the Lord at all times; His praise shall continually be in my mouth.' There in my pocket-book were three checks for my satchels—a thing I had never done before, as I always took them in the train with me.'

CHAPTER VI.

In Charleston, S. C.—His First Experience in Open Air Meetings, Together with Many Other Exciting Scenes and Narrow Escapes with His Life, Which He Passed Through in Prosecuting His Work.

His brother, Major Ed. Willis, and his sister, Mrs. Robert M. Adam, both being in Charleston, prevailed on him sometime about the years 1878–1880, to come down there, and for a time he claimed that as his home. He became a member of Trinity church. In 1878 Rev. J. S. Tuskip held a great meeting in this church. It had been in a cold, dead state.

Miller and a few others covenanted to meet and pray together for one hundred nights, or until God sent a revival. That was, perhaps, the longest protracted prayer-meeting on record. But the revival came. God sent it through John S. Tuskip.

Several hundred were converted and joined the church.

It was here that Miller first engaged in street meetings. He had some thrilling experiences. He was arrested by the police, but on application to the Mayor permission was granted him to hold the meetings. "At first," he says, "I stood alone in these meetings." Then his brother-in-law, R. M. Adam, joined him, and at the last, Thos. H. Leitch, now, and for several years past, an evangelist of great power. The Lord blessed these meetings. He says the Lord helped to talk, and men joined Trinity from the meeting, and all the stir was on that corner.

MEN CURSED HIM.

"When I began to hold these meetings," he says in the account he gives, "men cursed me and shook their fists in my face, and called me all the bad names they could think of. I was holding a meeting one evening when a dear man came up and said, 'The workman is worthy of his hire,' and gave me a silver dollar. The wicked men began to say I was paid to do this thing, so I threw the dollar as far as I could send it. Some little darkies picked it up. I felt real bad about it, and tried to find the good brother that gave it to me, but could not." He thought it compromised him with these wicked people; but he learned better afterwards than to throw money away that the Lord sent him. "Hallelujah to our God! there have been men who told me that that corner is the only place where they dared to hear the Gospel. Whether that be so or not, I tell it to the glory of God. 1st Cor. x:31." It seems from an entry he makes in his memorandum that the pastor there, Brother ———, told him he made folks nervous in the church. This is his entry in reply: "God knoweth the way I take."

HE IS KNOCKED DOWN BY A BARKEEPER.

"In Charleston, S. C., in 1879, one bright day, walking down East Bay, where I had often reproved or exhorted the barkeepers, one great double-jointed Irish brother walked out of his bar-room as I came along, and raising his great fist, struck me on top of the head, knocking me down. He hurt my neck quite badly. I walked on, but my neck pained me. At dinner I met my brother-in-law. He says, 'What's the matter with your neck?' I asked him who told him anything about my neck. He said he wanted to know what was wrong with me. I asked him if he could see that there was anything wrong with me, for then I was in pain, but did not want to say anything about it. I know what I would have done and what I would have said before God sanctified my soul. I'm afraid I would have out with my knife and used it, or attempted to; but I did praise God I was accounted worthy to suffer for Jesus' sake. Oh, hallelujah to God for the love that bears all things!" And yet there are some of our Bishops who say about this that none have attained it. According to their view, God has laid down rules that no man can follow. Now, reader, do you believe this? Isaiah 55 and 7, and also Isaiah 35 and 8.

HOW HIS WORDS WERE BLESSED TO THE CONVERSION OF A YOUNG MAN.

"Revival services were being held in Dr. ———'s Presbyterian church, in Charleston. Great crowds were going day and night. A young man asked me which car he must take to Dr. B.'s church. I told him he could take the red-light car and go to the bar-room, and the pleasure resorts, and to hell; or he could take the white-light car, and be in good company with serious folks, go to the Presbyterian church, and to Heaven by getting holiness, like Hebrews 12 and 14. This young man was converted that night, and when he told his experience, he said: 'I met Brother Willis, and he told me the red-light car would take me to hell, but the white-light car would lead me in the way to Heaven. So I resolved to-night, at any cost, to go to Heaven. God has converted my soul.' That was a word fitly spoken. 'Words fitly spoken are like apples of gold in pictures of silver.' To God be all the glory."

WRITING IN FRONT OF EAGLE ENGINE HOUSE, IN 1878, CHARLESTON, S. C.

" I was passing there one day, where there were a lot of drunken men. I had a piece of chalk in my hand. I stooped down on the flagstones and wrote: 'Come to Jesus now—prepare to meet thy God,' and walked on. He had gone about ten steps when the drunken crowd came out to see what I had written. Says one: 'Just see what the old crazy fool has written down here,' and they all took a hearty laugh over it. Three years after this I was up in a mission meeting, conducted by Brother Beard, a city missionary, when a man arose in the meeting and said: 'Brethren, I want to say a word. Three years ago, I and a lot of drunken men were standing in Eagle Engine House, when an old man passed by, crazy, as I then thought, and wrote on the flagstones in front of the engine house: 'Come to Jesus now—prepare to meet thy God.' I walked out and read them with the crowd, and laughed at and cursed the man who wrote them. But I could not get rid of them—day and night they followed me. I drank more and more, but these words haunted me. I resolved to get rid of them, by having a big drunk; so I told my wife not to bother me. I got a small keg of whiskey and put it by my bed. I would call my wife every now and then to fill up another bottle. After I had been drunk about twelve days and nights, I called for my pistol. I placed it, as I thought, against my forehead, determined to destroy myself. I pulled the trigger and shot the hair off the top of my head; the ball passed through the headboard into the wall. My wife came rushing in, thinking I was dead. But I awoke to my senses, and resolved there and then to 'come to Jesus' and 'prepare to meet God.' Brethren, I am a Christian to-day. The man who wrote on those flagstones is present in this meeting. I am happy in the love of God, and a good husband and father. If there is a man present who is nearer hell than I was, I should like to see him.'"

In the day of final reckoning hundreds of such cases will appear, I have no doubt, to the glory of God, and a crown of rejoicing to this holy man.

HOW DR. ——— GOT THE BLESSING OF SANCTIFICATION.

"Dr. ———, at Old ———, was a member of one of Brother ———'s churches, in ——— county, Georgia. Brother ——— was preaching a holiness sermon. Dr. ——— said: 'I cannot understand it.' Many brethren and sisters were entering into this rest of faith, like John xvii: 17; 1 John iv: 17. I said: 'Doctor, suppose all the church was shut up, not a ray of light could be seen in any part of it—suppose a window glass was taken out and covered over with black paper, so that not a ray of light could enter. The sun was shining brightly outside, and some one walked up with a needle and stuck a small hole through the black paper; immediately a ray of sunshine came through and you saw it. Now, Doctor, God will not give you a ray of light until you believe.' In an instant he said: 'I see it, and if that is it, I have got it.' The Lord filled his soul and he began to praise God. 1 John iv: 17-18—'Herein is our love made perfect; that we may have boldness in the day of judgment, because as He is, so are we in this world. There is no fear in love; but perfect love casteth out fear; because fear hath torment. He that feareth is not made perfect in love.'" Of all the other workers I ever knew he was the most untiring, as he was also the most successful in leading souls, either for conversion or sanctification, into the light. May the Lord raise up others like him in this respect, as well as in others.

BROTHER WILLIAM ———, AND HOW HE WAS CONVERTED.

"I was in ———. I was walking across ——— street one evening; Brother ——— was standing in front of his splendid house. I said, 'Brother ———, you have all that heart could wish for in this world—splendid home, good wife, good children. All this and Heaven would be glorious; but all this and hell would be awful.' 'What shall it profit a man, if he gain the whole world and lose his soul?' That talk in the hands of God, so Brother ——— said in a meeting where I was present, resulted in his conversion. All the glory to God; he has since been a useful member of the Presbyterian Church."

HOW HE SPOKE TO A MAN AND WHAT CAME OF IT.

"I was in ———, Ga., and Brother ——— was holding a meeting there. I was walking on the street and saw a brother riding in a buggy with either his wife or daughter, I did not know which, when I called out to him, 'Are you a converted man? Do you know if you were to die you would go to Heaven?' He drove on and made me no answer. Next morning I was walking down town, and I stopped in front of a blacksmith's shop, and said to the same man I spoke to in the buggy the evening before, 'Brother, there is an old book that says, 'What shall it profit a man, if he gain the whole world and lose his soul?' He says to me: 'If ever you speak to me on the subject of religion again, I will jump on you and break every bone in your body.' I told him he would break God's bones then, for I had turned my soul and body over to the Lord. I walked on down to the corner of the street, and then came back again, feeling that I was a coward. I walked in front of the shop again. I thought to myself, if they are God's bones, as you say, do your duty and fear not. I stood in front of the door and pointing my finger in the brother's face, in six feet of him, I said in rather a loud voice: 'Proverbs, twenty-ninth chapter and first verse, He that being often reproved hardeneth his neck, shall suddenly be destroyed, and that without remedy.' I stepped off again and had not gone far when I met Brother ———. I said to him: 'I spoke to a brother in a buggy on the street yesterday, because I felt the Lord said, 'Call out to him.' I did call out; but when I spoke to him again this morning he told me if I ever spoke to him again he would 'jump on me and break every bone in me.' I have spoken to him since then— just now—but I feel I must speak to him once more; now what must I say?' He replied: 'Go to him and say, Prepare to meet thy God!' I did so, and felt as clear as an angel of his blood. I left some days after. On the train — I think at the first or second station— they asked me, 'Have you heard the news?' I said 'No; what is it?' They said, 'You spoke to Brother ——— about his soul [he called everybody brother— Ed.] and he threatened to kill you; he sent out on the street this morning—said he wanted to see you and beg your pardon—that he was dying, and was going to Heaven; he had joined the Presbyterian church!"

HOW HE SPOKE TO ANOTHER MAN IN THE SAME TOWN, AND THE END OF HIM.

"As Brother ——— was walking up the street, I said, 'Brother, you are a man bound for the judgment.' 'Yes,' said he, 'and you go back to Augusta and attend to your own business. We have preachers up here, and, besides, I don't want any of your preaching to me on the street, anyhow.' I said: 'Woe to the man that putteth the bottle to his neighbor'—'woe unto him that giveth his neighbor drink, and maketh him drunken also, that thou mayest look on their nakedness.' He swore dreadfully that he did not want to knock me down. I said, 'Well, beloved, I am going to leave you. Prepare to meet thy God.' I left the town, and soon after I heard that he fell from his horse and broke his neck."

CONVERTED ON THE SPOT.

"Before I left ——— I was going on the street from the woods, where I used to go to be alone and pray. I saw a sister up in her porch. 'Sister, except ye be converted, and become as little children, ye shall not enter into the kingdom of heaven,' and pointing my finger at her as I spoke, I walked on. Next morning she stood up in Brother ———'s lovefeast, and she began to shout and praise the Lord. She said: 'A crazy man passed my house, and pointing his finger at me, said: 'Except ye be converted and become as little children, ye shall not enter into the kingdom of heaven.' She said: 'The spirit of God carried the message home to my heart on the spot, and the Lord has converted my soul.'"

CHAPTER VII.

A Continuation of His Work, Including Expe-periences that Remind the Reader of the Heroic Days of Methodism — A Policeman Waiting at the Door of the Church to Take Him to Jail.

"Brother ——— and myself dropped into ——— church. A brother walked up to me and said: 'Now, be quiet, for there's a policeman at the door waiting for you. If you do not keep quiet he will take you out.' I said, 'Brother, if God says be quiet, I'll be quiet as a mouse, but 'we ought to obey God rather than man.' He answered: 'You *must* be quiet *now*, or I'll call the policeman.' I looked up in the organ loft, and there were brethren with newspapers reading them, and walking about. I said: 'Suppose you go up stairs and quiet those brethren, and then come and regulate me.' I expect I slapped my hands a little too loud, whereupon one of the brothers caught them, saying, 'You must be quiet!' Seeing I would not be allowed to worship God according to the dictates of my conscience, I rose up and walked out. As I struck the street, the thought flashed all over me: 'You have done wrong to come out of the house of God for fear of man.' So at night Brother ———, Brother ——— and myself started back to service. I told them as we were going back, 'I am going to make all the noise I please this night.' I walked in and stamped as I walked in; slapped my hands. I had previously said to Brother ——— and Brother ———, 'here's one man who will be carried to jail out of a Methodist church,' when, to my surprise, the preacher came down from the pulpit and said to me: 'Here, Brother Willis, is a five-dollar bill; you may need a little money, as you travel around.' I said to Brother ———: 'I went to church yesterday morning in all good conscience to serve God, when I was threatened with being put in jail. I came to church to night with no single eye to please God, and the preacher came and shook hands with me, invited me to come and spend some time with him—the children, especially, wanted to see me and talk with me.' I left ——— thinking that it would take a man like Daniel to live in some churches without backsliding. But all glory to our God that we are down here in Florida, years afterwards, Isaiah xxvi and 3: 'In perfect peace, because our mind is stayed on God,' and we are trusting Him moment by moment. Hallelujah to our God. Amen!"

THE OLD MAN WHO JUST GETS SAVED IN TIME.

"Brother Frank Farris asked me to come down in Richmond county, near Augusta, and help him. One evening, about half-past five o'clock, we were going on our way to one of his meetings. We saw an old brother near the road plowing corn—the corn was about three and a half inches high, and it was tasseling out. Brother F. said to him, 'Don't you want to go to the better land?' The old brother said: 'I want to go to a better land than this,' pointing to his little corn. 'Well, we are having a good meeting over here at the Methodist church. Come over to-night.' The old brother came, and oh, what a sermon we had. Then Brother Farris asked all to come up to the altar to be prayed for. The old brother came, and the third night the Lord wonderfully converted him; he was happy for three weeks. He took sick and went shouting home to Heaven. He praised Jesus for the day that the two Methodist preachers come to ask him to meeting. 'Oh!' he says, 'I just got in in time.' Reader, how is it with you? Can you say like this poor old man, if you were called now, that you would be just in time? Second Corinthians, 6th chapter, 2d verse: 'Behold, now is the accepted time; behold, now is the day of salvation.' Reader, is this your experience?"

FAST TRAIN AND THE COLLISION.

"We were on the Georgia railroad from Augusta to Atlanta. The train was running from thirty to forty miles an hour. All at once there was a tremendous crash, and all of us were pitched forward on our faces, and oh! what a grinding noise, like timbers breaking to pieces. We were in the last car, and the back door was open. All the passengers, except one sister with a baby, and a young man, were out before I knew what was the matter. I stood up in the car and said: 'I am trusting in God, who are you trusting in?' I did not know but in one moment more we might go down through a bridge one hundred feet high on rocks or into the water. But I knew they who trust in God shall be as Mount Zion, which cannot be moved—Psalm 125 and 1st verse—and I did not think a railroad train could move a mountain; so I was in peace. Praise God for a peace that railroad accidents can't take away. Only the sister with the babe in her arms, and the young man, with myself, were left in the car. I said: 'Sister, I do not blame you for not jumping off, but why did you not jump off, young man?' 'Oh, I was paralyzed.' 'Well, you are not to be blamed either,' I replied."

HE SPOKE TO A YOUNG MAN ON THE STREETS IN AUGUSTA.

A few days after, this young man and a young lady were out in a boat on a mill pond, when the boat capsized and they were both drowned.

DEATHS IN ATLANTA.

He speaks of several deaths in Atlanta during the months of June and July, 1890, soon after he had spoken to them the word of the Lord.

WHY HE RECORDS THESE REMINISCENCES.

I find this entry in his blank book: "There is but one reason for writing these thoughts. Perhaps there

may be some one in my condition, and they may help him. Pray over each page, and God grant they may be a blessing, is the prayer of your less than the least brother—1st Thes. 5 and 23.   S. MILLER WILLIS,
Greenville, Fla., Madison county, Jan. 16, 1890."

Also this entry: "For fear when I die it may not be in writing when I was sanctified, I write it now in my Bible: Converted in 1864, and sanctified the sixth day of October, 1877, thirteen years after. All glory to Jesus for it. Your less than the least brother—1st Thes. 5 and 23.   S. MILLER WILLIS."

"SANCTIFICATION AND HOW I GOT IT."

"I sought it like Mark xi: 24. 'Therefore, I say unto you, what things soever ye desire, when ye pray, believe that ye receive them, and ye shall have them.' I received it at White Oak church, while Brother Dunlap was preaching from Ephesians iii: 14 to 21. 'For this cause I bow my knees unto the Father of our Lord, Jesus Christ, of whom the whole family in heaven and earth are named. That He would grant you, according to the riches of His glory, to be strengthened with might by His spirit in the inner man ; that Christ may dwell in your hearts by faith ; that ye, being rooted and grounded in love, may be able to comprehend with all saints, what is the breadth, and length, and depth, and height ; and to know the love of Christ that passeth knowledge, that ye might be filled with all the fullness of God. Now unto him that is able to do exceeding abundantly above all that we ask or think, according to the power that worketh in us, unto him be glory in the church by Christ Jesus throughout all ages, world without end, Amen.' I thought if God was able to do all that, surely He is able to sanctify a little fellow like me and in a moment the Lord came into my soul and drove 'the buyers and the sellers out,' and filled me with that xxii in Mathew, beginning at 37th verse: 'Jesus said unto him, 'Thou shalt love the Lord thy God, with all thy heart, with all thy soul, and with all thy mind.' This is the first and great commandment, and the second is like unto it. 'Thou shalt love thy neighbor as thyself.' On these two commandments hang all the law and the prophets. I made all hear me, saying, 'I know when I was converted like Mathew xviii and 24. 'Except ye be converted and become as little children, ye shall not enter into the kingdom of heaven.' Yes, I got converted, and that as bright as any living man ever was. Oh that I may be faithful unto death, and the Lord has promised me a crown. Rev. ii and 10. And if there are starry crowns, I want one of them, too. But a more excellent way was for me, and I sought and found it after my conversion, to the joy and consolation of my soul, in I Thes. v and 23. I found after conversion I could not answer in my own heart such as 2d Corinthians, seventh chapter and first verse: 'Having, therefore, these promises, dearly beloved, let us cleanse ourselves from all filthiness of the flesh and spirit, perfecting holiness in the fear of God.' That passage, as Brother ———— would say, came to me and showed me there was something wrong in me. I heard Brother ———— tell how he was convicted for a pure heart. He was a medical man before he was a preacher. One day as he was riding along, his horse stumbled, and it made him mad. He struck the animal with his whip in the eye and put it out. 'There now,' said he, 'if I had been a Christian I would not have done that; there is something wrong inside.' Then this wonderful passage came to him and he said: 'I am not cleansed from all filthiness of the flesh,' or I would not have struck my horse that way.

"When I heard him tell that, I said, well, some of our good brethren say they got it all when the Lord converted them. I knew I did not, and the Lord gave me the second blessing, as Mr. Wesley says, 'properly so-called.' I knew if I could bring to bear the required faith, I should have the 'second benefit.'—2d Corinthians, 1 and 15. Oh, hallelujah! and Amen! and praise the Lord! for the 'second benefit' of entire sanctification! or perfect love; or holiness, as in Isaiah xxxv and 8, 'And a highway shall be there, and a way, and it shall be called the Way of Holiness.' The unclean shall not pass over it, but it shall be for those; the wayfaring men, though fools, shall not err therein.' Mathew fifth and eighth calls it a 'pure heart.' No matter what we call it, if we hold fast to Bible terms.

But let us stand by the 'law and the testimony,' remembering what Jesus said—'If any man be ashamed of Me and my *words*, of him shall the Son of Man be ashamed when He shall come in His own glory, and in His Father's, and of His holy angels." See Luke ix and 26.

CHAPTER VIII.

His Visit to the ——— Circuit, North Georgia Conference, and the Work of God in That Charge While He Was There—Taken from His Memorandum Book.

"1880. A crazy man! With Brother Dunlap around ——— Church. Brother D. preached, and oh, the opposition at first. But it soon gave way under the power of the Holy Ghost. In the beginning of the meeting no word was too bad to be used against any one who professed to be sanctified, nor did they hesitate to destroy their property; and I guess, like one of old, they thought they were doing God's service. Some one went to a buggy belonging to Dr. ——— and cut his dashboard to pieces. He said not a word of condemnation. Nearly all thought I was a crazy man. Dr. ——— invited Brother Dunlap and me to go spend the night with him. We accepted the invitation, and were treated like princes."

HOW DR. ——— AND HIS WIFE AND SON GOT SANCTIFIED.

"About midnight we heard a knock at our door, then the voice of Dr. ———, saying: 'Oh, brethren! get up! get up!' Brother D. got up, and then I. 'What's the matter, beloved?' 'Oh,' said the Doctor, 'I cannot sleep; I am in great darkness; I must have this question settled; I cannot live in this state; I must have light, and have it now.' We began to pray, first one and then the other, Brother ——— taking his turn with us. Finally, while I was praying, the light began to break in, and he cried, 'I've got it! I am a sanctified man!' Then we three praised the Lord like the men of old. Acts xvi and 25: 'And at midnight Paul and Silas prayed, and sang praises unto God, and the prisoners heard them.' Well, Sister ——— heard us, and so did her oldest son; they both came rushing into the room. Now, the Doctor wanted his wife to enjoy the same experience. We began to sing and pray with her, and Jesus, according to His word, Matthew xxi and 22d verse: 'And all things whatsoever ye shall ask in prayer, believing, ye shall receive,' was faithful to His promise. We asked the Lord to sanctify her, and He came in mighty power and did it. John xvii and 17th verse: 'Sanctify them through Thy truth; Thy word is truth.' She cried and praised God, too. Things were getting noisy now; but not greater than Acts, second chapter, and from first to fourth verses: 'And when the day of Pentecost was fully come, they were all with one accord in one place. And suddenly there came a sound from Heaven as of a rushing, mighty wind, and it filled all the house where they were sitting. And there appeared unto them cloven tongues like as of fire, and it sat upon them, and they were all filled with the Holy

Ghost, and they began to speak as the Spirit gave them utterance.'

"The thirteenth verse of second chapter of Acts says: 'Others mocking, said: These men are full of new wine.' This is about what the good people about ———— said of Brother D. and myself, until the Lord raised up witness after witness to praise and bless God that 'in the twinkling of an eye, Jesus's blood can sanctify.' Yes, whosoever can say with their whole heart, 'Trustingly my all I give,' will be able to say, experimentally, 'Perfect cleansing I receive.'

"Hallelujah! This is my experience. When I gave up all, Jesus came in and took possession of my poor soul."

DR. ———— DID NOT THINK HE WAS CRAZY.

"When we went to church next day the brethren all wanted to know of the Doctor what he thought of the crazy man. 'Brethren,' said the noble Christian gentleman, 'I was the crazy man.' Since that time his precious wife has gone home to heaven in great triumph. Mr. Wesley said in his day: 'Our people die well.' But a greater than Mr. W. has said—Psalm xxxvii: and 37: 'Mark the perfect man, and behold the upright, for the end of that man is peace.' Yes, bless God, peace to live with, and peace to die with. A peace that flows like a river. I know I have Second Corinthians fifth chapter and first verse: 'For we know that if our earthly house of this tabernacle were dissolved, we have a building of God, an house not made with hands, eternal in the heavens."

THE ARBOR.

"Brother D. and I went to ———— Arbor, about twelve miles from ————, in ———— county, Ga. (A Methodist church has since been built here. The incidents he relates occurred in 1881.—ED.) We talked to all freely about their souls. A brother came to us and said: 'You and Brother D. have been talking to my father, a man old enough to be your father, and the best Christian in all this country.' Brother D. told him he had no idea of talking to him, but he came to us and wanted to know if we could give him any light on the great subject of entire sanctification. We told him it was all embraced in the words of Jesus, Math. xxii and 37: 'Thou shalt love the Lord thy God with all thy heart,' etc. As we talked to him the Lord came upon him in mighty power. Acts. i and 8. He fell over in the straw and shouted aloud the praise of Jesus." (This was Brother ————, and, sure enough, he was one of the most consecrated men in the N. Circuit. But he was a great slave to the use of tobacco, and had never had any conviction of its filthiness until he received the light of holiness. Although he was past fifty years of age, he gave it up without a moment's hesitancy, and I have heard him say since, often, if sanctification did no more for him than to save him from tobacco, it was worth all it cost to get it. His dear sister, Mrs. ————, got gloriously sanctified during this meeting, and gave up her pipe, after being a slave to it for many years. She so lived and demonstrated it in her life as to convince many gainsayers of its truth. She died a few years since, a bright witness to the glorious experience of perfect love and entire sanctification, as a subsequent work of grace to regeneration, received and lived by simple faith in Jesus. But we will let Miller continue his narrative.—ED.) "One M. D. got the experience after this manner. He said it was not for him, for he had sought night and day, but could find no peace. 'Oh,' said he, 'if I could be happy like you people, then I would tell it too.' I said: 'Doctor, if you had a patient under your care, and you were to give him three different medicines, and he were to take one or two, but declined to take the other, saying he did not think it was the right kind for his case, what would you say to him?' 'I would say, get another doctor, for I can do you no good, if you will not obey my orders.' 'Doctor, you obey Jesus, just as you require your patient to obey you, and you shall have the sweet peace to come into your soul.' He came to the altar and said: 'I do now and forever give myself to God, and here and now I claim Matthew, first chapter and twenty-first verse: 'Thou shalt call His name Jesus, for He shall save His people from their sins.'' I said: 'Now, Doctor, you can believe, can't you?' 'Yes, yes.' 'Well, then, make a profession of your faith, like Hebrews, tenth chapter and twenty-third verse.' He said: 'I can, I will; I do believe that Jesus saves me now.' But it was not until the next morning, while he was in the very act of confessing the Lord Jesus as his sanctifier, that the witness came into his heart by the Holy Ghost that he was wholly sanctified. Oh! what a stir it created. About forty, more or less, were saved under that bush arbor; praise our Jesus for it. Some of them stand to-day, hallelujah and praise to our dear Redeemer! Some of the workers, and some of those who sought and found peace, have moved to their mansions above. Since those bright and happy days Sister H. and Sister M. can look down from their home on high and see many who, when that bush arbor meeting commenced, were on their way to death and hell, but are now marching for heaven."

A MAN WHO COMES TO CHURCH TO MOCK IS SUDDENLY SEIZED WITH AWFUL CRAMP ALL OVER HIS BODY.

Many thrilling incidents occurred during the series of protracted meetings held this year on the N. Circuit, while Brother Willis was with me. I will relate one or two. It was at ———— church. A man came out one Sunday. Many had been stricken down by the power of the Holy Spirit, and had either professed conversion, or was seeking—while some believers had been sanctified; but this man had made his brags that he could not be moved by any such fanaticism. He took his seat in the back part of the church, and began in every possible way to show his contempt for the service, except by some overt act which would amount to an open disturbance. About the time penitents were being invited forward he was suddenly seized with a physical spasm. His body was drawn into almost every conceivable shape. He fairly bellowed from pain. He was carried home in that condition, and a physician was sent for, but medicine seemed powerless to relieve him. He sent for Brother Willis and myself. We prayed for him, but it was far into the evening before he obtained relief. Brother Willis made this laconic remark: "Well, he came to make fun, but he nearly got killed."

NEARLY TURNED OUT OF DOORS.

We went to a prominent church in the ——— circuit. After service one of the best and principal men of the church invited me home with him, and of course I took Miller with me. This brother had a son who was himself a Primitive Baptist, and he had married a wife who was out and out on that line. They were living in the house. Miller, of course, as usual, had a word for every one. This good woman could not bear him in her sight. She went to her husband and told him the two could not stay in the same house—"either that crazy fool had to go, or she would." He went to his father, and the dear old brother came to me. He protested his regrets, but said Miller would have to go. I said: "All right; if Miller Willis can't stay here, I can't either." Certainly I did not blame the dear old man, but I did pity him.

THE BROTHER WHO CLAIMED THAT THE HOLY SPIRIT HAD LEFT HIM.

The most remarkable case of this sort I ever knew occurred in one of our meetings, or rather was discovered, for he had been in that condition for years, so he claimed. A brother, intelligent, educated, an examplary member of the church—would pray in public, was a kind, loving husband and father, and yet he believed the Holy Spirit had left him.

Brother Willis and I labored with him—prayed with him publicly and privately, but seemingly all to no purpose. His wife was a consecrated, holy woman. He loved Miller, and would do any thing he said. I have known them to spend hours in the woods together, at Miller's request, but the brother never manifested any feeling; all he did was mechanical; he said he had no feeling. I never saw Miller Willis more drawn out for any man. He always believed the brother was under a most powerful temptation of the enemy. For years he wrote to this dear brother, and as long as he lived he prayed for him.

If these lines should fall under the eyes of that brother or his saintly wife, they will know who I am writing about, although I call no name. They are among my dearest friends on earth, and our sainted Miller will expect to meet both of them in Heaven.

SALEM CAMP-MEETING.

Miller went with me to this camp-meeting on the ———— Circuit. Dr. Jesse Boring was the Presiding Elder. Brother Willis created a sensation, you may depend, as he always did, on his first arrival. Dr. B. gave him the right-of-way, and he soon won the best people on the encampment; but, as everywhere, he captured the children first. In 1881–2, I was stationed at St. P., in Atlanta. Miller came to help me as usual. This was his first visit to the city, where he afterwards had some thrilling experiences, as related by himself and Brother M. D. Smith. He soon became greatly beloved by the best people in the church, and was instrumental in the conversion, reclamation and sanctification of some who will meet him in Heaven.

CHAPTER IX.

WITH REV. E. B. REESE, ON FAIRMOUNT CIRCUIT, NORTH GEORGIA CONFERENCE—AN ACCOUNT OF THE WONDERFUL WORK OF GRACE ON THAT CHARGE AS RELATED BY HIMSELF, TOGETHER WITH AN ARTICLE WRITTEN BY REV. W. A. PARKS, AND PUBLISHED IN THE "WESLEYAN CHRISTIAN ADVOCATE."

There was no man among us whom he delighted to be with more than Rev. E. B. Reese, of the North Georgia Conference. In the fullest and best sense, they were "true yoke fellows." No one sustained a greater personal loss in the kinship of twin spirits on earth than Brother Reese when Miller left us. No one knew both the inner and the outward man of Miller Willis better than Dr. Reese. He came all the way from Watkinsville to Augusta, in response to a telegram, to attend his funeral. No one could have written the true life of our sainted brother better than Brother R.; indeed, he can furnish data which no one else can, and I had relied on him for at least one chapter in his life.

I will give such facts as I find in Miller's memoranda. The record as I find it, is confined to the years 1881–'82, when Brother Reese was on the Fairmont Circuit. These were pentecostal years in Brother R.'s ministry, and he attributed his success largely to Miller Willis being with him.

There was great opposition to the preacher and his helper, on account of the doctrine of Holiness, which they preached and urged with great boldness, both publicly and privately. While there was more or less of this from some who were in the Methodist Church, it come mainly from members of other churches. But these men of God pressed the battle to the gate, and stirred up the devil generally. So bitter was this spirit for a time that they found some difficulty in finding a place at which to stop. But they lived on their knees, and the result was, the power of God bore down all obstacles before them.

The revival fire broke out all over the circuit, and hundreds were converted and added to the church, while the standard of holy living was lifted to an attitude such as had hardly ever been known before, while some believers were wholly sanctified. Such is the uniform result of the faithful preaching of Bible holiness. Mr. Wesley bears testimony to it in his day; the fathers of American Methodism in theirs, and we see from the New Testament what it did for the world in the beginning; and blessed be God, some of us know in our own experience and observation that the Holy Ghost honors such preaching as he honors no other. Oh, that He would restore to Methodism this distinctive characteristic of her early ministry.

But it comes only to those who pay the price. Hear

him: "We went to Fairmount, Gordon county, Georgia—Brother Reese and I—to *preach, teach* and *live* holiness. We were told 'No use to go—every door in the place is closed against you.' We got down in the woods and cried to God, on our knees, for help—like the Psalmist in thirty-fourth Psalm and sixth verse: 'This poor man cried, and the Lord heard him, and saved him out of all his troubles.' We soon found an open door for our entertainment. The dear brother and sister were very kind to us." One of the first meetings they held was at Wesley Chapel. He says: "Presbyterians and Baptists came for miles to hear the new doctrine, as they called it. We told them it was the Bible doctrine. The most spiritual of all the churches came to our meetings. The little church was filled to overflowing, and all around were men and women who could not get in. People came out who had not been to church for years. They came to see and hear the crazy man, as many of them called me. They looked at me with amazement. Frequently Brother R. and I would jump out through the windows at eleven and twelve o'clock at night, with the house still full of people shouting and praising God. Fifteen and twenty would be converted at one service. One man came to Brother R. and said: 'You are a young preacher, and just beginning to make a name for yourself. Now, I want to tell you: the best men, and the most influential, in all this country have whiskey made, and take their drams; my advice to you is to go slow in your raid against whiskey making and drinking—don't tear the church all to pieces and ruin your own prospect.' Brother R. told him they could not retain people in the church who were in league with the whiskey devil. Here was a test, but Brother R. told them lovingly they must either quit the evil or quit the church. The brother above referred to had something better in store for him—his wife was a consecrated Christian, and she got wholly sanctified; the result was the Holy Spirit reached his heart in mighty power. He was reclaimed from his fallen condition, and then gloriously sanctified."

THE MAN WITH A WHITE HAT ON.

"The church was packed as long as standing room could be had, with the doors and windows full. I said to Brother R., 'Do you see that man with the white hat on?' he said, 'Yes.' 'Well, that man is grieving the Holy Spirit, First Thessalonians, fifth chapter and nineteenth verse, and Genesis sixth and third.' I put out my hand toward them and cried out, 'There is some one grieving the Holy Spirit in that crowd.' No sooner had I spoken than out jumped the white-hatted man, he being the only one who moved. Two young sisters from a hard-shell family came and joined the church. After being converted, under the power of the Spirit they would skate along on the floor like they were on ice; then they would stop and praise God at the top of their voices like the others. From here we went to Pine Log Church, in Bartow county, Ga., and such a time as was there! Old and young were converted. Some infidels were convicted and brought into the church, and became useful members."

A WONDERFUL REVIVAL.

Rev. W. A. Parks, P. E. of the Dalton District, North Georgia Conference, for the year 1881, writes to the *Wesleyan Christian Advocate* in October regarding this most wonderful revival in the Gordon Circuit:

"There are five churches in this charge—Rev. E. B. Reese, pastor. Most of the churches are in the eastern part of the county—Old Pine Log is in Bartow. They have been in what may be termed a revival state for the last four months. Some of them held protracted meetings for three and four weeks, and then after a rest of a few weeks, they commenced again. Though there have been over one hundred conversions and accessions to the church, this, in the estimation of many, is a small part of the work accomplished. More persons have professed entire sanctification than have been converted. Brother Reese and his co-laborer, Miller Willis, have directed their labors in behalf of holiness for the last four or five months. In the beginning of their efforts many even of the Methodists derided, while the Baptists persecuted, and the world laughed. But these faithful men, themselves wholly consecrated to God, toiled on in faith until the power of the Holy Spirit overcome all opposition. Gray-headed men and women profess to have received new light, and been led into a higher life.

Young men and maidens, boys and girls, profess to have received sanctification. Some Baptists who at first scorned the work, have sought pardon, and then have gone on to profess holiness of heart. Men and women, who never spoke in public before, walk the floor back and forth, exhorting sinners to flee the wrath to come. One rather remarkable characteristic of the meetings is, there seems comparatively little shedding of tears or shouting, and as soon as a believer professes heart purity—whether man or woman—they go at once to preaching, or, in other words, to exhorting the people as on the day of Pentecost. The Gordon Circuit is full of preachers. They preach on the highways, in the social circle, in the sanctuary, and everywhere. There are constantly new conversions, and professions of perfect love are common at the prayer-meeting and the home altar. It must be known, too, that many of these churches have been in a cold, backslidden state, and considerable discipline had to be resorted to. The pastor does not realize the extent of the work, and says it is only just begun."

Brother Willis relates these further incidents: "An old preacher came to Brother R. and said: 'You would do great good if you would get rid of that man, alluding to me. Why he is crazy; I have seen many like him.' But Brother R. did not think so. At one of our meetings a sister came to Brother R. and told him not to bring me to her house. Soon after that at a morning meeting she sprang up from where she was kneeling and began to exclaim: 'Oh, I'm sanctified! I'm sanctified! Now, Brother Willis, you can come to my house.'"

As long as Miller lived there was no place at which he was more at home than at the house of Dr. Reese, and as long as he was able to work, he delighted to be with his dear friend and brother, Dr. Reese. What a shout there will be when these two meet in heaven.

CHAPTER X.

MILLER WILLIS AND THE HOLINESS MOVEMENT.

He was no polemic in any critical sense of that term. He would not controvert. He made no pretentions to scholarship. He wrote brief reports sometimes of meetings, but a regular communication for publication he never wrote that I ever heard of; but, in a large degree, so far as Georgia is concerned, he was the inspiration of the Holiness movement. It incarnated itself in Miller Willis. He was the most dogmatic man I ever knew. He never tried to prove God's Word to be true. He said it was so. He never hoped he was converted, he *knew* it. He never hoped or believed he was wholly sanctified, he *knew* it. I have often heard him say, "I know I am converted better than I know my right hand from my left, and I know if I were to die this moment, I'd go straight home to heaven." "He overcame by the blood of the Lamb, and the word of His testimony."—Rev. xii: 11.

MILLER WILLIS AND THE HOLINESS MEETING.

If there was one place on earth that Miller regarded as next to heaven, it was the holiness meeting. He was perfectly at home here. He could do as he pleased, and say what he pleased. He had a universal habit of clapping his hands, and crying out amen, when anything suited him. Sometimes he would find himself in a church where this gave offense, both to the preacher and to the congregation. But in a holiness meeting he was perfectly free.

The main reason, however, why he enjoyed such meetings was, because he believed that holiness was the only thing that embraced the whole Gospel. Not that he despised or neglected the lower forms of Christian experience, but because rather, he believed that very few possessed a Scriptural experience of conversion unless his conviction for sin, and repentance, were founded on the Scriptural doctrine of entire sanctification. So that from the beginning—like the Wesleys—while he saw that men are justified before they are sanctified, yet "holiness was his aim." Here, then, from John Wesley's standpoint, he felt he was on solid rock in advocating and attending definite holiness meetings. There has been of late years much opposition to these meetings. The opposition has arisen from one of two reasons—either because they were misrepresented, or because the one who opposed was not a Wesleyan Methodist. Miller Willis was none of your modernized Methodists—he was Wesleyan against the whole world. He believed John Wesley was the greatest man since the days of the Apostles. He never wasted his time in reading anything that contravened the Wesleyan view of entire sanctification. He was "rooted and grounded" in both the doctrine and experience.

THE HOLINESS MEETINGS AND THE STREET MEETINGS.

He was a power in a street meeting, and the street meeting was wonderfully effective as conducted by these red-hot men and women. There are men on their way to heaven now, that I could call by name, who would be in their sins and on their way to eternal death but for the open air service during a holiness meeting.

Miller was given to saying startling things. I have known him to startle a whole congregation as if a bomb shell had suddenly exploded in their midst. He gloried in striking a blow at formalism wherever he got an opportunity. This was one reason for his breaking over all seeming proprieties while the preacher was preaching sometimes, either by stamping with his foot, clapping his hands or crying out: "Who's believing?" Then, again, "Who's praying?" Or, yet again: "Who's ready to die if he were called this moment?" Pity the preacher who might be preaching a dry, dead sermon with Miller Willis in the congregation. He'd either have to catch on fire or quit in despair. The preachers had no better friend, or one that was more jealous of their rights. Sometimes a red-hot message from him would result in the pastor getting his support in full. At another time it would result in a new parsonage. One of the best parsonages in the ———— Conference was hastened to completion by a single word from Miller. It was during a holiness meeting. The pastor was very much in love with his people, and they with him. They had a good church and a six hundred dollar pipe organ, but they had a leaky parsonage for their pastor to live in. They intended to build a new one, but they were slow about it. Miller didn't like it. The pastor was one of his favorites, anyway. While the pastor was up before an immense congregation on Sunday, saying some nice things about his people, all at once Miller cried out: "Oh, yes, you are mighty clever! Yes, you are clever enough to buy a six hundred-dollar organ for your church, and let your preacher live in an old, leaky parsonage!" The shot went straight to the mark. Men and women resolved with one accord to roll away that reproach at once, so that every new pastor that lives in that splendid house, owes it in a sense to Miller Willis.

"TIE THAT STOVE TO MY FEET OR I'LL GO UP."

In all my intimate association with him I never saw Miller Willis lose his head under religious excitement. He often did things and said things that looked and sounded to those who took a cold-blooded view of every thing, like the doings and sayings of a crazy man. But in the midst of any sort of a spiritual cyclone, when every body seemed to be in a whirl, he could in a moment, and with a steady hand, take a dead aim with the Gospel bow, (his gun never "missed fire") and he but seldom failed to bring down the enemy. "Retreat or fall back" were words he never learned from the "Captain of his Salvation."

A brother tells me of his first seeing Miller; it was at

Gainesville, Ga., during a Holiness meeting; Dr. Watson was present and conducting the service. Every phenomenon was present that characterized the first Pentecost, except the noise of the descent of the Holy Ghost and the visible tongues of fire. No man can appreciate this Pentecost who is not in sympathy with the first. Miller, along with others, was caught by the glorious influence. He shouted to the by standers, "Tie that stove to my feet, or I shall fly away to Heaven!" Of course, the strange brother, who, while himself in perfect harmony with the whole scene, had never heard it after that sort before, and very naturally, the first thought was, "well, that's a wild man." But, he afterwards learned by close intimacy with him, he was anything but a 'wild man,' except on the same sense that St. Paul said he himself was, "a fool for Christ's sake."

CHAPTER XI.

MILLER WILLIS AS A BIBLE STUDENT.

Miller Willis was preëminently a man of "one book." Not that he did not read other books, for he did. But for twenty-five years his reading all tended in one direction—the knowledge of God as revealed in His Word, together with an all-consuming desire for wisdom to win souls to Christ. As he was unique in all else, so was he in his methods of studying the Scriptures; many references have been made in these pages by different writers or speakers, to his Bible. I knew him most intimately in this part of his Christianity. Besides reading the Scriptures consecutively through from Genesis to Revelation, he studied the Bible topically. To this end, he carried with him everywhere he went a copy of Cruden's Concordance. He would take, *e. g.*, the word repentance, and collate every passage that had that word in it. Then he would take some other word—faith, perhaps, and go through the same exercise with it. So he went through the whole book, not once, but no doubt hundreds of times, giving the preference, of course, to those words that related most directly to salvation and a holy life. Is it any wonder that he was perfectly at home in the Scriptures, and that the most learned theologian found a match, aye, more than a match whenever he presumed to controvert with Miller about the two great facts of the Bible—sin and salvation? Then again, it is no marvel that his quotations are so universally accurate, or that he always gave the book, chapter and verse. Above all, he believed the Bible; he did not try to explain away its meaning to suit his views. He did not set up a standard of his own, either in doctrine or experience, and then go to work to bring its teachings down to correspond with this, but he sought to know the Bible standard, and then bring his experience and life up to that.

MILLER WILLIS'S BIBLE AND ITS REMARKABLE MARGINAL NOTES.

Miller Willis's Bible.

How shall I describe it? I doubt if there is another like it. I do not mean, of course, the book in itself as the Bible, though even this is unique, but I mean the notes, the comments, the personal application of certain passages, together with the general make-up of the book. It is interleaved with blank paper, on which very many things are written, all, however, relating to doctrine, experience or the Christian life.

To get a correct idea of the contents of this book—I mean the things written in it by Miller Willis—one must see it and read it for oneself, but I may be able to give the reader of this some conception by a few quotations.

We take what is first written on a blank leaf in Genesis vii and 1; Heb. vi: 7: "Noah stands against the whole world for God. By faith, Noah being warned of God of things not seen as yet, moved with fear prepared an ark for the saving of his house. Noah believed God was going to destroy the world. The men around him laughed him to scorn. We may go out of the world and yet have it in us—it must die out of our hearts first.

Holiness.—"Why (does) the regenerate need entire sanctification? Because of the nature he has inherited.—Genesis vi: 5. Because of the work begun in regeneration.—1 Cor. iii: 1-4. Because of his conscious need of it.—Ps. li: 5-8. Because God hath enjoined it.—1 Peter i: 16. Because God hath provided for it.—Heb. xiii: 12. Because it is a possible grace for the present life.—Luke i: 74-75. Because of its greater power for service. Contrast the case of the Disciples before and after Pentecost. Because it is a way so much better.—Ps. xxxv: 8-10. Because the world needs such kinds of examples and testimonials, just as it needs witnesses and examples of converted men; because it is essential to enter heaven.—Heb. xii: 14. Because a holy heart is the best."

In answer to this question: "Is any thing too hard for the Lord?"—Gen. xviii and 14—he answers: "Yes; I am too hard for the Lord, if I don't repent, for he says "except ye repent ye shall all likewise perish."

Genesis xxii: 18: "Do I obey the voice of my God? Help me to from this day, September 1, 1890."

Genesis xx: 35: "Judah means praise the Lord."

POWER! GENESIS XXXII: 28.

"Thomas Harrison calling, and they coming from the galleries. Pleasant Grove camp-meeting—men fell like dead men. These that have turned the world upside down have come hither also. What a soul-winner the Apostle John was! What power Peter had when the Holy Ghost fell on all them who heard the word! Under the preaching of Luther, how the world was swayed. Knox, with his burning words, set fire to Scotland, and made the Queen tremble. John Livingston preached a sermon, and they prayed all night, when five hundred were converted.

"We are weak in public because we are weak in the closet. We don't pray in secret like we preach in public. 'Oh, mind how you loose your inward peace,' Gen. xlii and 21. Math. xxvii and 4: 'This tells you what others dare not whisper in your ear; consider the nature of your present actions, they are seed sown for eternity, and will grow when you are in the dust.'

"Exodus iv and 12th: 'Well send me my God, if you will be with my mouth, for then I know I shall think and speak right.' Exodus viii and 10: 'And he said: To-morrow.' A young man at a camp-meeting was entreated by several to come to the altar and get saved. He said: 'No; not to-night, but to-morrow.' Next day the leader said: 'Where is the young man who said last night he would seek God to-morrow?' A young man came forward and said: 'He is at home dying—a raving madman.' Be sure, the last call will come soon.

"Exodus ix and 28: 'See how God can send the mighty thundering to alarm the wicked.' Exodus xv and 26: 'I am so glad he did not say Moses was to heal me, for Moses is dead; but he said: I am the Lord that healeth thee.' Exodus xxxvi and 7: 'Is this the way I give to the Lord?' Deut. vi and 25: 'Nothing in the Bible but what is conditional. Ask and ye shall receive.' But suppose I don't ask—shall I receive? No, no. But men say, 'I can't do anything.' 'If I do not believe I shall be damned.' 'What shall I do to be saved?' 'Believe on the Lord Jesus Christ, and thou shalt be saved.' Read twenty-seventh and eighth chapters of Deuteronomy, and see how God can curse a man, and then how He can bless. Joshua i and 8: 'This Bible is a book of *doing*, and not simply believing. The Acts of the Apostles is what they *did*, as well as what they believed.' Joshua i and 14: 'Oh, my God, make me a mighty man of valor!' Joshua iii and 5: 'Thou shalt be perfect with the Lord.' If the Lord had said, 'Miller, you must be perfect with men,' I would say, 'Lord, your Son could not do that.''

"Joshua xiv, last clause of 8th verse: 'But I wholly followed the Lord.' Can I say amen to this? Lord, help me! Yes, praise the Lord! 'Waycross, Ga., Nov. 24th, 1890. Brother Waller: One hundred and fifty converted up to date, and fifty-odd sanctified.' Praise God for it. Ps. xxxiv: 1st verse.

"Joshua xvii: 17-18: 'For thou shalt drive out the Cananites, though they have iron chariots, and though they be strong. What does our God care for iron chariots or strong men? He can lock the wheels so they cannot move, then send dismay to those who drive them.' Dukes, Ga., December 11th, 1890.

"Judges viii: 4. 'Faint, yet pursuing.' 'Lord, help me to pursue until death!' 'Do I believe Samson threw down the house on the Philistines? Yes, for my God says it in His word. Judges xvi: 28-30." I find this on a blank leaf in his Bible: " A brave Congo boy, about twelve years old, was rowing a boat for his mother. She saw something in the water and stooped over to see what it was, when a monster crockodile seized her and jerked her overboard, and swam away toward an island with her in his mouth. The boy followed as fast as he could. He found his mother lying on the bank, while the beast had gone off to look up its mate. He rescued her and brought her away in safety. Was this boy worth saving? Well, there are hundreds of thousands like him."

"Why are my prayers not answered?" Ps. lxvi and 18. "Can I say this?" Ps. lxix: 9. "For the zeal of Thine house hath eaten me up; and the reproaches of them that reproached Thee are fallen upon me."

"They that trust in the Lord shall be as Mt. Zion, which cannot be removed, but abideth forever." Ps. cxxv: 1st verse.

Here is his comment, taken in part from Bishop Simpson's sermons: "Methodism has not grown by money from the public treasury. The Roman Catholic and Reform Churches, the Church of England, the Church of Scotland, the Romanist, and Presbyterian of Ireland have all had public money; also, the Episcopal and Congregationalist were supported partly at public expense, but Methodism has stood alone. The Methodists have trusted in God for all they got, praise the Lord for it. They had to learn self-reliance. The Lord is round us while we sleep, and, like the mountains, when we wake He is still there. 'Why do my thoughts wander when I pray?' Prov. xxiii: 26. If you would keep your heart fixed on God, and realize to yourself by faith His holy and awful presence it would not be so. If the President of the United States came to see you, would your mind and heart wander from His presence and words? would you be light and trifling? 'All things are naked and opened unto the eyes of Him with whom we have to do.' Heb. iv: 13. 'Can you say to the Lord, now Lord, I am sowing to the Spirit?' Mr. Finney says he never found one man in a thousand that knew what was meant by giving their heart to God! They know what it is to give their hearts to their wives—that it means to do everything to please them."

"'Son of man, can these bones live?' Ezekiel xxxvii: 3. 'The Prophet answered: O, Lord God, Thou knowest.' 'As much as to say with man it is impossible. So without God man cannot be saved. Is there any earthly remedy that can make these bones live? The Prophet looked at the bones. They were very dry. What supernatural work has been done in your heart?

And you know it is of God. Nothing but repentance toward God and faith in the Lord Jesus Christ on your part, can bring about such a work. Any view that teaches that man is not ruined, that the whole heart is sick, the whole head faint, is false. If this is not so, why make superhuman efforts to save him? An aggressive Gospel always says man is ruined. 'Knowing, therefore, the terror of the Lord, we persuade men.' My God, help us! If we did not believe in a supernatural power, who would go out into the field to preach? But the mighty God who made the bones before they were dry, says go, and promises to 'Breathe on these dry bones.'"

"THE TWO FIRES." MATH. III: 11-12

"The Fire of the Judgment, that consumes eternally, or the Fire of the Holy Ghost, that consumes sin and saves the soul, which will you choose? My God, help me!"

"Blessed are the pure in heart." Math. v: 8. "The sisters, when they go to clean their houses, throw all the windows open, and let the light in. Then they scrub and scrub as long as they can find a speck of dirt or a cobweb. Now they are ready for company, and if they find anything afterwards, they scrub again." "Whenever a justified soul ceases to hunger and thirst after God, the light goes out, and they simply have a name to live, while they are dead. There are thousands all over the country in this condition. Why can't we feed the people? Because they are not hungry. If you set me down to a table loaded with all that is good to eat, and I have no appetite, I will not do it much harm." See Math. v: 6.

"Many will say to me in that day, etc." Math. viii: 22. 'Many think themselves Christians who are not, for Christians are holy, these are unholy. Christians love God, these love the world. Christians are humble, these are proud. Christians are gentle, these are passionate; consequently they are no more Christians than they are archangels." John Wesley.

"Who can tell a Methodist from a ball goer, or theater goer? A young girl dying, a member of a church; her friend, member of another branch, came to see her. She was shocked when she saw how near death she was, and knew how worldly she had been, and yet she did not realize her true spiritual condition. When her visiting friend tried to talk to her, she said: 'Oh, your people think these things are sinful, but my church does not.' She grew weaker and weaker. At length her friend was obliged to leave her, but the sick girl seemed to get brighter and brighter; so she said to her friend, 'let me put on my shroud and see myself in the glass before you go.' But when she come to the sight of herself, all at once she began to cry out, 'I can't die! I can't die!! Then I won't die!!!' She screamed at her preacher, 'Oh, thou deceiver of men!' and died.

"Has the Lord any use for me? Well, He needed an 'ass,' and sure He can make some use of a man, if he will only be passive in His hands, like the 'ass.'"

Math. xxi: 1-11. "Jesus was asked which is the great commandment? and answered: 'Thou shalt love the Lord thy God with all thy soul, and with all thy mind.' Math. xxii: 37-40. I am satisfied He knew which was the greatest. Mr. Wesley says this is holiness. This is perfect love. This is entire sanctification."

"January 10th, 1891, Dukes, Ware county, Georgia. A father left his boy and said, 'now, be patient and do your work well.' Rev. x: 11. 'Be thou faithful until death and I will give thee a crown of life.' The father said to his little boy, 'I will come soon.' When the little fellow would get up in the morning, a thrill of joy would go through his heart, because, he said, 'Papa may come to-day.' One day he did come. His boy threw down the broom and ran to meet him. The father opened his arms and embraced his child. 1st John, iv: 17: 'Herein is our love made perfect, that we may have boldness in the day of Judgment.' Here is the secret of dying grace!

"Now, let us take the last written in the book: 'Will you be a Christian now?' 'Am I now a Christian?' Math. xviii: 3; 'How do I know it?' 2d Cor., v: 17, also Rom. viii: 14-15-16; 'Am I backslidden?' Rom. viii: 1, also 1st John, ii: 15; 'Am I ready to die?' Luke xii: 36; 2d King, xx: 1; Amos, ix: 12; 'Does Jesus save me from my sins now?' Math. i: 21; 'Shall I obey my Lord now?' Math. v: 48; 'Am I going to miss Heaven?' Heb. xii: 14.

"'Am I sanctified throughout soul, body and spirit?'

1st Thes. v: 23; 'Am I a man of God like this?' 2d Tim. iii: 17; 'Have I obeyed this command of my Savior?' 1st Peter, xv: 16; 'Shall I have boldness when the world is on fire?' 1st John, iv: 17; 'Am I cleansed like this?' 2d Cor. vii: 1; 'Does the truth sanctify me now?' John, xvii: 17; 'Have I obeyed this scripture?' 2d Cor. vii: 1; 'When can I be saved from all sin?' Ans.: 'Behold, now is the day of salvation,' 2d Cor. vi: 2; 'For we know if this earthly house of our tabernacle were dissolved,' etc., 2d Cor. v: 1.

"Search the Scriptures carefully for the above.

"Reader, many will die deceived, Math. vii: 22-23.

"Thirty thousand promises in the Bible, eighty-two for each day. Praise the Lord."

I beg to close these extracts by presenting to the reader an epic poem, which I know is well worth its space. I find it in his Bible, and I have often known him to use it with powerful effect on a congregation. I do not know the original author of it, but E. P. Marvin is credited with it in its present revised form.

THE THREE BIDDERS.

An Incident in the Life of Rowland Hill.

Just listen a moment, dear friend,
   And a story I'll unfold—
A marvelous tale of a wonderful sale,
   Of a noble lady of old.
How hand and heart in an auction mart
   Her soul and her body she sold.

'Twas in the king's highway so broad,
    A century ago,
That a preacher stood of noble blood,
    Telling the poor and low
Of a Savior's love, and a home above,
    And a peace that all might know.

A crowded throng drew eagerly near,
    And they wept at the wondrous love
That could wash away their vilest sins,
    And give them a home above;
When lo! through the crowd a lady proud
    Her gilded chariot drove.

"Make room! make room!" cried the haughty groom,
    "You obstruct the king's highway;
My lady is late and their majesties wait,
    Give way there, good people, give way!"
But the preacher heard and his soul was stirred,
    And he cried to the rider, "Nay."

His eye like the lightning flashes out;
    His voice like a trumpet rings;
" Your grand fête days, your fashions and ways,
    Are all but perishing things;
'Tis the king's highway, but I hold it to-day
    In the name of the King of Kings."

Then he cried, as he gazed on the lady fair,
    And marked her soft eye fall:
"Now, here in His Name a Sale I proclaim,
    And bids for this fair lady call;
Who will purchase the whole, her body and soul,
    Her coronet, jewels and all?

Three bidders already I see—
    The World steps up as the first,
'My treasures and pleasures, my honors I give,
    For which all my votaries thirst;
She'll be happy and gay through life's bright day,
    With a quiet grave at the worst.'

Next out spoke the Devil and boldly bids,
    'The kingdoms of earth are all mine;
Fair lady thy name with an envied fame,
    On their brightest tablets shall shine;
Only give me thy soul and I give thee the whole,
    Their glory and wealth to be thine.'

And what wilt Thou give, O sinner's true friend;
    Thou Man of Sorrows unknown?
He gently said, 'My blood I have shed,
    To purchase her for mine own.'
To conquer the grave and her soul to save,
    I trod the winepress alone.

I will give her my cross of suffering here,
    My cup of sorrow to share;
Then with glory and love in my home above,
    Forever to dwell with me there;
She shall walk in light in a robe of white,
    And a radiant crown shall wear.'

Thou hast heard the terms, my lady fair,
    Offered by each for thee;
Which wilt thou choose and which wilt thou lose,
    This life, or the life to be?
The figure is mine, but the choice is thine,
    Dear lady, which of the three?

Nearer and nearer the preacher's stand,
　　The gilded chariot stole;
And each head is bowed as over the crowd,
　　The gospel accents roll;
And every word which the lady heard,
　　Burned into her very soul.

"Pardon, good people," she kindly said,
　　As she rose from her cushioned seat;
As the crowd made way, you might almost say
　　You could hear her pulses beat;
And each head was bare as the lady fair,
　　Knelt low at the preacher's feet.

She took from her hand the jewels rare,
　　The coronet from her brow;
"Lord Jesus," she said, as she bowed her head,
　　"The highest bidder art Thou;
Thou hast died for my sake and I gratefully take
　　Thy offer—and take it now.

I know the pleasures and treasures of earth,
　　At best they but weary and cloy,
And the Tempter is bold, but his horrors of gold
　　Prove ever a fatal decoy;
I long for Thy rest—Thy bid is the best;
　　O Lord, I accept it with joy!

I turn from the pride and ambitions of earth,
　　I welcome Thy cross now so dear;
My mission shall be to win souls for Thee,
　　While life shall be spared to me here;
My hope ever found with Thee to be crowned,
　　When Thou shalt in glory appear.

"Amen!" said the preacher with reverent grace,
   And the people all wept aloud;
Years have rolled on and all have gone,
   Who around that altar bowed;
Lady and throng have been swept along,
   On the wind like a morning cloud.

But soon, O how soon, the glory and gloom
   Of the world shall pass away;
And the Lord shall come to His promised throne,
   With His saints in shining array;
May we all be there with the Lady fair,
   On that Coronation day!

CHAPTER XII.

A Short Chapter Giving a Few Samples of Miller's Letters, Together with Some Answers from Correspondents.

The life of Miller Willis would be incomplete without a specimen of his letters. Striking in everything he did, perhaps it is conspicuous nowhere more than here. I never saw, heard or read of any one who wrote in the same style he did. Religious—scriptural—yes. His entire letters were ofttimes one continuous quotation from the Bible, giving always book, chapter and verse.

He not only faced the enemy himself, but he was ever ready to stand by, uphold and encourage others to do the same. A few years ago when Dr. W. A. Candler had the conflict with the theatrical mistress and her admirers, in Nashville, Tenn., Miller heard of it, and while it greatly rejoiced his heart to know the young minister was standing for the purity of the church, he sat down and wrote him a letter, an extract of which is here given—only an extract, for the original is too highly prized by Dr. C. to be turned over, except to copy. Also see Dr. C.'s reply:

"Warrenton, Ga., ——, 1887.

"Dear Brother Candler:—Heard some were in for driving you from your position about the Love of the World. Oh, stand fast in the liberty wherewith Christ has made you free. Oh!!! LIVE IN THE 13TH OF 1ST COR., and hold on to God. Then fear not, beloved. They told me your position and the opposition. I said he will be there when you hear from me again. God bless you and Sister Candler; tell her I never hear of her these days. She will have to live in earnest to get up to some of the women in the Bible, or in Augusta, either. Brother Candler, be all love like the blessed 13th, then fear not. Your less than the least but loving brother, 1st Thess., 5 and 23. S. M. WILLIS.

"Not that I am competent to advise you—but a word fitly spoken—'like apples of gold in pictures of silver.' God bless you and yours."

"NASHVILLE, TENN., Oct. 28, 1887.

"MY DEAR MILLER:—I judge you are at Cedartown. If not the brethren will know where you are. So I send this note there. I thank you for your brotherly words. The Spirit led you to write them. They did me good. God hears you when you pray—pray for me. I need wisdom and grace for His faithful service. You understand how I am situated. Ask our Father to help me. Wife joins me in love to you.

"I am, yours affectionately, W. A. CANDLER."

SEVERAL LETTERS TO CAPT. W. T. TERRY, OF ORIENT, NEW YORK.

Capt. Terry was a seafaring man. He followed the sea before the war between the States. He owned and commanded a merchant ship that plied between New York and Charleston. I am indebted to him for several letters written to him at different times by Bro. Willis. Brother Terry is himself a very intense Methodist of the Wesleyan type. His vessel was named, "The Rev. John Fletcher." This name in itself would attract Miller Willis, for, next to John Wesley, he admired John

Fletcher as one of the Methodist fathers. But there were other remarkable facts connected with this sea captain and his ship. He had a ship's crew that neither drank whisky, used tobacco, drank coffee or tea, or used profane or vulgar language. In other words he was a Christian seaman, commanding a Christian ship, with a Christian crew. Capt. T. and Miller became acquainted in this wise: Capt. T., as was his custom when in port, was attending church, and when in Charleston he always attended Trinity M. E. Church, South, the church to which Miller belonged while he lived there. He heard Miller's hearty responses during the services, and mentally said to himself, "That brother has the right ring, I must see him as soon as worship is over." They met, a look into each other's eyes, and a word of self introduction, and they were friends, not only for life, but for all eternity. It was a clear case of "love on first sight." From then on, whenever they were in C. together they were almost inseparable.

The following letter, without any date, I judge to be among the first he wrote Capt. Terry. It must have been in 1878, as that was the year, I think, of the great revival at Trinity, conducted by John S. Inskip.

Dearly Beloved Brother Terry:

Oh! Charleston, yes, Charleston! the formal city, the church city, where men know more than their teachers. Who can teach a man wise in his own eyes? But, bless the Lord! oh, my soul, will shout for a little. Men, that a few weeks ago, scoffed at us and spit upon Holiness, now they are leading a life hid with God. Oh, cry aloud to God to shake the South from center to circumference, Amen; it will be done, glory! glory!! Amen. Bro. Terry, this is the greatest meeting since the days of Mr. Wesley, in Charleston. Was not altogether friendly to the means at first; did not like the way it was presented; thought was too much compromise for men of God; but, the best men of the church were the first to seek it at the altar— Amen. Some seeking conversion, while others sought perfect love round the same altar. Up to date, so far as rough calculation goes, about 300 or more have been converted; about 75 or 80, perhaps one hundred, sanctified. My brother, for whom I have prayed fifteen years and six months, was converted. I promised the Lord never to rest until my wicked brother was converted and saved from all sin, until he was made perfect in love. Thought I would shout aloud if he ever went to an altar, as he was a leading spirit among the men of the world. Thought, "Oh, give it up," *No, never!* will die saying, "*Will not let thee go except Thou bless me.*" But satan says, "asking *too much!* men like your brother, a leader among men, *Oh! no, never!*" But enough, Amen! Beloved Bro. Terry, he did go up to an altar, and cried to God to have mercy on him, and he is still saying farewell to his old companions. Many bad men have met me saying, "Is your brother seeking religion?" "Yes, he is, praise the Lord for it, and so ought you." Oh, my Brother has been too proud to yield, having been an officer in the city, a leader among the wicked, a president of a fire company. Men said to me, "Will give him three weeks to come *back.*"

The balance of this letter did not come to me, but I will add, that the evil prophesies concerning his brother did not come to pass; he is still faithful to the vows he then took upon himself. If ever one brother idolized another, Miller idolized his brother Ed. Ed. being the oldest, and Miller the youngest, and his father dying while he was young, had much to do in bringing this about, I have no doubt. But he was ardent in his affections, and grace made him more so.

But to return to his letter to Capt. Terry. Capt. T. used to send him a great many religious magazines, papers and tracts. The following seems to have been written in acknowledgment, with thanks, for a supply of these:

"CHARLESTON, S. C., 1879.

"Read, Beloved, the 37th Psalm, and each time you read, ask the Lord to bless all the errands of love sent out for Him. Thanks; yes, ten thousand thanks. The Sunday-school papers for all, little and older ones too. A stray shot from the Word lodged in some heart may be a star in your crown. Can't tell you all in a short letter. Came home from the ship that brought the papers, etc., after trying to talk to Capt. P., but he was in great hurry, did not even have time to hear what was a Christian! but, what of that; gave some papers to the young man aboard, perhaps the mate; said he would read them. Oh, Beloved, we here in our day are not called to do like Peter—*walk the water*. What! yes, walk the water. Well, Abraham was not far behind that, for his son, his only son, he was to do that horrible act (Oh, Lord, help now) take his life. Oh, we can't all be like George Muller, trust for two thousand children to be fed and clothed. Now, Bro. Terry, let us take from the 19th verse in 6th chapter of Matthew. How can we ever doubt that our Father will feed and clothe us after reading that. Thank the Lord! for fifteen years I have wanted no good thing—no, nothing. Listen to this: 'When I sent you out without purse or scrip, lacked ye anything? They say, nothing.' Oh! shout, Bro. Terry; you have lacked nothing; I have lacked nothing, Amen. Luke, xxii: 35. Read it, Beloved. 'Yours less than the least.' I. Thes., v: 23.

"S. M. WILLIS.

"P. S.—'Rejoice evermore, and in *everything* give thanks. Whatsoever is not of love, forgive.' S. M. W."

"CHARLESTON, Jan. 17, 1880.
"*Dearly Beloved Brother Terry:*

"Oh for the blessed promises of the Bible—listen now: 'They that wait upon the Lord *shall* renew their strength.' The Bible, the blessed Bible! 'Be ye holy' just *now*, for see 'tis in the present tense. Oh, beloved, the Bible is full of it. Listen to Jesus, 'Be ye therefore perfect, even as your Father in Heaven is perfect.' *Amen! Amen!! Amen!!!* Reading in the last number of the *Earnest Christian* that letter from Brother R. Gilbert, I could have shouted Amen to each word. He is right. Let men preach perfection as clear as Mr. Wesley did. Tell the sisters not to wear gold and costly apparel, then look out for opposition from the worldly professors of religion. Tell them they must be perfect—they must be holy or miss Heaven—and you will surely get your share. But what of it—'They that will live godly *shall* suffer persecution.' How is dearly beloved Brother Terry? Does he stand a *witness* of perfect love or not? Good-bye, dearly beloved brother. Oh, be a witness for Jesus that perfect love casteth out fear. When the storm rages then sing, 'I'll trust the covert of His wings.' Isa. xxvi:3. Now read 2d Cor. xiii:6.

"Yours in love, S. M. WILLIS."

"CHARLESTON, S. C., 1881.
"*My Dearly Beloved Father and Brother Terry:*

"Long months since I have written my dear father and brother. When I first received your dear letter, wrote and mislaid a long letter; searched for it, then said, 'Perhaps the Lord allowed it to be lost,' so am writing this. Do you remember your dear little schooner?—'Rev. John Fletcher'—when we prayed on board of her here in Charleston, S. C.? Brother S. B. Goodell, S. M. Willis, and, I forget, but believe no one else but you were there—Amen. Since then, believe we both are happier and more like Jesus. There is a disposition in Trinity M. E. Church, South, not to be definite on the great doctrine of Perfect Love, but the Lord has done wonders here on the line of temperance.

"Go on, my beloved father; talk Perfect Love, sing Perfect

Love. The longer I live the more I think what a great man Mr. Wesley was. Writing long time ago he said: 'There is a general faintness come upon the whole land on this Bible doctrine of Perfect Love.' Lord, wake up Methodists *North, South, East* and *West* on our *Life*, for perfect love is *the* life of Methodism. We ought to be counted by millions upon millions— I mean those who profess *Perfect Love*. No other person should be called a Methodist. Your son and brother,

S. M. WILLIS.

"P. S.—Whatever is not of love, forgive. 'Rejoice evermore, and in everything give thanks.' S. M. W."

"HAVE FAITH IN GOD."—Mark xi: 22-24.

MANATEE, FLA.

"Praise God, my precious brother, Capt. Terry. Hallelujah to Jesus, we are both still alive. Your letter reached me after a time—had to go to Charleston, then to Spartanburg, S. C., and then all the way down here nearly into the Gulf of Mexico. Get your map and see where Manatee, Fla. is, and that is where your least brother is. I was about to die with hemorrhage, when some of the brethren gave me the money and told me to come down here. Well, this is not the place, as it is too damp. My precious brother, can you say my heart is just right with God? and you have the witness? Acts vii:21.

"Well, praise the Lord, there have been one thousand conversions, Mathew xviii: 3, and sanctifications, 1st Thes. v: 23. It is not the old time, red hot, Holy Ghost conversions, where they jump up as on springs and go after friends, with the glow and the burning zeal that lasts for weeks; but its the best we have, and we are going to say amen.

"When asked: 'Do you know you are converted?' 'Yes.' 'Have you got the happy in your heart?' 'Yes.' 'Are you going to tell your friends about it?' 'Yes.' But they used to tell all this themselves. Three hundred in Dalton, Ga., three hundred in Waycross, Ga., and the rest in Douglassville, Augusta and Atlanta, Georgia. Praise God! Let us be filled with joy, though the world take fire, Nehemiah vii: 10; 1st

Thes. v: 16. Brother Terry, do you rejoice evermore and pray without ceasing? God bless you, and may your last days be your brightest. The sixth chapter of Nehemiah tells just the way men talk to-day against the work of our God. Had one hemorrhage in Waycross, Ga., and another the night after it. I was then so weak I could not walk fifty feet, but, amen to God, Mathew vi: 10. I am still alive, and expect this summer, God willing, to see some tall sons fall under the power of the Gospel. How about your ship, Rev. John Fletcher? What of her crew, who neither swore, used tobacco, drank whiskey, beer or coffee? The air here is laden with the perfume of orange blossoms, and there are plenty of oranges, too.

"My post office is Augusta, Ga., care of Brother Josiah Miller, 432 Green street. I am hardly ever there—nearly always off at meetings somewhere. But now am nearly done for. Brother Terry, you ought to know where the money comes from, Luke xxii: 35, lacked nothing. Praise God for one hundred and third Psalm and first verse. Write and tell me all about yourself. Good-by, my precious Brother Terry.

"Your less than the least brother, 1st Thes. v: 23,
"S. MILLER WILLIS.
"March 5th, 1891."

Below we give, as we suppose, the last letter he ever wrote; indeed, he did not write it; he only dictated it, for it is not his handwriting—it is the writing of a lady, one of his nieces no doubt:

"SPARTANBURG, S. C., June 9th, 1891.
"Mark, xi: 22-24.
"MY PRECIOUS BROTHER TERRY:—You see I am in the upper part of South Carolina, and though I am so weak I can hardly stand on my feet, my soul is all on fire for God and the salvation of lost men. That tract you want, you can obtain of Brother M. D. Smith, Lavonia, Ga.

"Arn't you glad it's written, 'Call unto me and I will answer thee, and will show thee great and mighty things which thou knowest not'? Jer. xxxiii: 3. Shout! Shout! Shout!!!

my dear brother, 'For eye hath not seen, nor ear heard, neither have entered into the heart of man, the things which God hath prepared for them that love him,' 1st Cor. ii: 9. I mislaid your letter; you asked some questions I intended to answer. But keep full of love and faith and you need fear nothing. Oh, hallelujah! full of faith like Heb. xi. Good-by, Gen. xxxi: 49: 'And Mizpah, for he said: The Lord watch between me and thee, when we are absent one from another.' 'Finally, farewell; be perfect," 2d Cor. xiii: 11.

"Your less than the least but loving brother,

"S. MILLER WILLIS."

The following tribute was sent to me by Major Willis, simply headed *Miller Willis*, and with the initials E. W.:

MILLER WILLIS.

Every good life leaves in this world a twofold ministry—that of the things it does directly to bless others, and that of the silent influence it exerts, through which others are made better or inspired to do like good things. Influence is something, too, which even death does not end. When earthly life closes a good man's work ceases. He is missed in the places where his familiar presence has brought benedictions. No more are his words heard by those who ofttimes have been cheered or comforted by them. No more do his benefactions find their way to homes of need where so many times they have brought relief. No more does his gentle friendship minister strength or hope or courage to hearts that have learned to love him. The death of a good man in the midst of his usefulness cuts off a blessed ministry of helpfulness in the circle in which he has dwelt. But his influence continues. The influence which our dead have over us is ofttimes very great. We think we have lost them when we see their faces no more, nor hear their voices, nor receive the accustomed kindnesses at their hands. But in many cases there is no doubt that what our loved ones do for us after they are gone is quite as important as what they could have done for us had they staid with us. The memory of beautiful lives is a benediction, softened and made more rich and impressive by the sorrow which their departure caused. The influence of such sacred memories is in a certain sense more tender than that of life itself. Death transfigures our loved one, as it were, sweeping away the faults and blemishes of the mortal life and leaving us an abiding vision in which all that was beautiful and pure and gentle and true in him remains to us. We often lose friends in the competitions and strifes of earthly life, whom we would have kept forever had death taken them away in the earlier days when love was strong. It is true, " He lives to us who dies; he is but lost who lives." Thus even death does not quench the influence of a good life. It continues to bless others long after the life has passed from earth. E. W.

He also says: He printed many thousand tracts—had a press of his own. One read: "Where do you expect to spend Eternity?"

Another: "Can you answer me this question: If you were to die this day, would you go to Heaven?"

To those who remember the fearful earthquake in Charleston in 1885, the following letter and reply will explain itself:

[COPY.]

"SEPTEMBER 2, 1885.

"MY PRECIOUS BROTHER:—We just learned from the morning papers you have had a violent and destructive earthquake. I have an abiding faith that neither you, nor yours, nor anything belonging to you has suffered any serious damage; 37 Psalm. Love to all the darling children and Sister Lizzie.

"Your affectionate brother, S. M. W.
"To Major E. Willis, Charleston, S. C."

MAJOR WILLIS TO THE EDITOR.

"My family were away except my eldest son, who slept through it all. My house was only slightly damaged, while the one above me was a wreck and the one below me very much injured. Yours,

September 21, 1891." E. WILLIS.

CHAPTER XIII.

Miller Willis' Scrap Book.

I have said in another place that he was a man of "One Book," and explained what was meant by that. I propose to give in this chapter a sample of his reading outside of the Bible. If the writers of any of these quotations should find them here, and be disposed to complain because their names do not appear, let me say, I copy them as they appear in Miller Willis' scrap book, sometimes with the author's name and sometimes without; and as I shall not insert any piece as original, I shall not give any name, but all that is in this chapter, it will be understood, are such things as he culled from books, papers and magazines. Nor do I use one-tenth of what he left in this form. If I were to include everything, it would make a much larger volume than this life of him. I have discovered a few short pieces of his own writing, including a short letter to the *Way of Life*, which I place at the end of this chapter.—ED.

Solomon says, "He that winneth souls is wise;" and Daniel, "They that be wise shall shine as the brightness of the firmament; and they that turn many to righteousness as the stars, for ever and ever;" and James says, "Let him know that he who converteth the sinner from the error of his way, shall save a soul from death and shall hide a multitude of sins." However we may look at this subject, it is of immense importance. Next to the salvation of our own souls, nothing should be of such importance as the salvation of our fellow men and women. Every soul touches at many points the interests of others. Each has relatives, friends or acquaintances, for whose spiritual welfare we are responsible before God. It is not by neglecting the duty, or forgetting it, that we can get quit of the responsibility; this can only be done by discharging it. When Jonah ran away from the presence of the Lord, he thought to get away from the responsibility of warning the Ninevites; but after all the dangers of his journey, no sooner was he upon dry land than the word of the Lord came again to him to go and cry against Nineveh the cry that He would put into his mouth.

Comrades, this responsibility rests upon us—the responsibility of the salvation or the damnation of souls. How important then that we should have the wisdom of winning souls.

It is not my purpose here to dwell upon the Holy Spirit's agency in this solemn business; this has often been done in these columns. I wish to dwell upon the

SOUL TO BE WON rather than upon the Divine agency which saves the soul.

The soul is not a faculty or an attribute; it is not thought, volition, memory or judgment; it is that which thinks, which wills, which remembers and which reasons. It is that which makes our individual personality. It is the *ego*—the I myself of my being; it is the imperishable, the indestructible something by which we live, and move, and have our being. It is that which is accountable, and which will have to give account to God. The soul is from God, and returns to Him, and may I not say that it is of Him—a partaker of the Divine nature. Its connection with the body is only an imprisonment; for its aspirations and desires are ever beyond that which can be whilst in the body. Its thirst for knowledge, power, fame and happiness is always beyond that which can be acquired in the body. Its susceptibility of enjoyment is beyond the body's power of endurance, and a "wounded spirit who can bear."

This wonderful personality in every man and woman we find sin-smitten, perverted and condemned to death. Its *thoughts* about God, holiness and eternal life are thoughts of indifference or of contempt. Its *will* is at enmity with God for no justifiable reason; it owns to be at a continued hatred to God's law. Its *memory* is the store-house of its rebellious weapons against truth and righteousness. Its *judgment* is in antagonism to God and His Christ. And yet this soul has been loved with an everlasting love. Christ died to redeem it

FROM SIN, death and hell, and you, my comrades, are called upon to win it. You are called upon to win it from the power of the devil; win it from its own inherent suicidal proclivities. Wild and mad it hurries on to destruction, like an unbroken and maddened horse. Stop it; save it; win it! Win it from itself and the power of the devil to Christ and its God.

Oh, what a work is this! Well may we say, "Who is sufficient for these things?" As the work is looked at from our side it appears impossible, but "With God all things are possible."

"He that *winneth* souls is wise." Does not this phrase seem to indicate the way the work has to be done? Let us not forget that we have to do with a soul which *thinks*, and thought is as free as a bird. We have to do with a *will*, and this will is like a wild, restive horse, which has not been broken. We have to do with a *memory*, and herein we have little to help us; and we have to do with a *judgment*, and this believes that we have chaff and worse than chaff for it; it believes that we have only what will make it miserable. WIN IT!

Can it be done by the rough plan of coercion? Can you make the will submit itself to your direction, or to the authority of a creed, and then flatter it with an easy future of indulgences? Can it be done by the thunders of "You SHALL do this, or ———?" by the threats of punishment either of this life or the life to come?

The plan is indicated by this word, winneth. This was Christ's plan. By the power of love and truth we are to win the will and convince the judgment and save the soul from DEATH. If we win a soul for Christ, we must do it in Christ's way. The main citadel of the soul is the will; carry it, and we can then lead the soul captive to the feet of Jesus. All our wisdom and our plans must be made to bear upon this point. Get it in any way that opens—through the reason, the affections, the senses, the passions or the memory. Convince the reason of the enormity of sin, of its wickedness, of the justness of God's plan in punishing transgression. Appeal to the affections; show them the love of God in Christ; show them that "God was in Christ reconciling the world unto Himself, not imputing their trespasses unto them. 2d Corinthians v: 18. Bring the power of the death of Christ upon their hearts. Appeal to their fears. The terrors of hell are an awful reality. Paul said: "Knowing the terror of the Lord, we persuade men." With your soul filled with a Divine pity, knowing the eternal danger of the unconverted, warn, reprove and rebuke, AND give neither yourself or your hearers rest until they are safe. Make no apology either by softened tone or remark. If the glories of heaven are real, so are the terrors of hell. Salvation is a reality, but damnation is none the less so. Beseech them to be reconciled to God. Gratify the senses. Give them plenty of good music; let them see and hear that you are happy in God, and urge them to "taste and see that the Lord is good." Deal with the memory. Find out who of them have had pious parents; remind them of home, and of the happiness which they had before they left for a life of sin. Use stirring literature. Put the *War Cry* into the hands of those you cannot otherwise approach. *Do not forget that you can accomplish nothing until you win the will. Mine and counter-mine.* With all the "*wisdom of the serpent*" approach this stronghold, with complete dependence on the Holy Spirit. *Never rest until you win the will,* then you will soon "*save a soul from HELL and cover a multitude of sins.*"

HOLINESS—SWORN OVER TO GOD.—Paul says: "I know in whom"—not in WHAT, but in WHOM, a person—"in whom I have believed, and am persuaded that He is able to keep that which I have committed unto Him until that day." Paul was a committed man from the moment of his conversion right on to his martyrdom. He was committed to God just as a young woman when she marries commits herself to her husband, and becomes amalgamated with his interests; and if she is a good and true wife, and has a good and true husband, she becomes one in spirit with him; she has no separate interest henceforth forever. In their children, money, business prospects, purposes, living and dying, they become one. It would be preposterous for any one to come to her and talk about setting up a separate interest from that of her husband. She would say, "You must be a lunatic, or think that I'm one. No, no; I am committed to live and die with him while he is a good and true man." Exactly in the same real and practical sense the true saint is committed to Jesus Christ.

NOW THAT IS FAITH, AND THERE IS NO OTHER FAITH THAT SAVES.

All other faith will delude and damn if you trust to it. There is no other, and we will, by God's help, sweep every other idea of faith from the earth. We will show the people what Jesus Christ meant when he said, "He that believeth in Me shall never perish." No, such people will never perish. How can they when they are committed to God? He will sooner let the archangels perish than He will let them perish. But the people who have a shilly-shally faith, who believe and work themselves into a bit of feeling, and sometimes think they believe, and sometimes think they do not—these are not the people who have the faith that saves. They have a faith of the imagination, a faith of the feelings; but they have never BEEN COMMITTED TO GOD. See them committed to Him to the extent of a $50 note! See if they are committed to Him to the extent of one of their children! The way to find out whether people are committed to God or not, is to see what they will give for Him, what they will do for Him, and how they will hold and use what He has given them for His sake and for His service.

You go to seek a situation, and you say to the master, "Well, now I am ready to serve you for such and such a salary." You make a bargain with that man, and he supposes, of course, that you commit yourself for the time being to his interest. He never supposes that you are going into his establishment, or into his family, to seek your own interest. He supposes that you are to be committed to him and his interests for the time being, and if you are not prepared to be so you are a dishonest man or woman, and you have no business to take his wages.

The real saint commits himself to God's interest for both worlds, for time and for eternity—forever; so that when God asks for your money, you say, "Here it is, Lord." When He asks for your children, you say, "Here they are, Lord." What a hypocrite I should have been, having professed these twenty-four years to be consecrated to the Lord, if I had withheld my children from Him when He wanted them. Is not any man or woman acting thus equally so, and yet I know plenty of parents in England who are loud-professing saints, or, at all events, take a high position in the Christian world, who know as well as I do that God wants their children for this war, and yet I believe they would sooner see them in their coffins than they would give them to it. I say God writes them down hypocrites. Mind, it is not I that say it—THEY KNOW that God wants their children to help us roll this Salvation war around the world, and they won't give them up. Tell me such people believe savingly in God! I would as soon believe it of the devil. Oh, no, no! we will sweep this sort of faith off the earth, by the grace and help of God. We will have a practical faith, or none

at all, and I challenge any divine, interpreting the
Scriptures in harmony with themselves, to show me any
other faith spoken of or illustrated in the New Testa-
ment, or in the experience of the Apostles, or the early
Christians. No other kind of faith is worth two cents.
If you have not got that faith—get it at once.

YOU CAN HAVE IT.

We are not going to talk about consecration—we
hope most of you are consecrated, and yet that involves
faith. I was thinking about Elisha when he parted
with Elijah, and when Elijah's mantle had fallen upon
him—then came the test for Elisha's faith. What is he
going to do with Elijah's mantle? How is he going to
show his faith? What would have been the use of the
mantle unless he were willing to receive Elijah's voca-
tion—unless he were prepared to endure the hardships,
the self-denials, the sacrifices, the dangers and persecutions which awaited him as a brave prophet of the Most
High? But you know that when Elisha took Elijah's
mantle he took Elijah's spirit and Elijah's calling; he
was going straight back again to Jordan to show that he
had taken it, and when he got to the banks of the river
he did not trust to his mantle or in any supposed consecration, but he showed the reality of his faith in the
living God by saying, "Where is the Lord God of
Elijah?" He acted out his faith; he dared to do the
works of Elijah; then the strength of God was given
to him, and you know he divided the waters and went

over. Now that is the test of faith—accepting the work of faith, obeying the call of God; accepting the consequences, the suffering, the cross—even if it should mean death. *That is faith. Those worthies in the 11th of Hebrews all showed their faith, not by their professions— though they did profess it—but they proved its genuineness by what they did and what they suffered.* "*They wrought righteousness, subdued kingdoms, stopped the mouths of lions; they were sawn asunder, they were afflicted, persecuted, tormented—of whom the world was not worthy.*"

Now, when we have a faith like that, the world will believe us. When we show the world our faith by our cross-bearing, our trial, our suffering, of whatever kind God calls us to endure, whether behind the scenes or before the scenes; in our hearts, or bodies, or circumstances; with our children, or with our money, or with our labor, or with our reputation, or in whatever particular department we are called upon to suffer—when we show this to the world, the world will believe us. Now, my friends, my comrades, will you seek this faith this morning? I said to a lady a little while ago, who came to me lamenting her condition, and telling what she wanted the Lord to do—"Suppose the Lord Jesus were here in His flesh, and you were telling Him what you are telling to me; supposing He were to turn round and say to you—'Oh yes, I am quite willing that you should follow me, and to give you all that you ask of me, but remember that the Son of Man hath not where to lay his head. Are you willing to follow me in poverty, in

9

trial, and in suffering, if the interests of my work require it?' What would you say to him? Would you say, 'Yes, Lord!' Have you the consciousness within you that your heart would answer, 'Yes, Lord!' Now, that is committal. He does not tell you where He will lead you, or what He will want of you. He does not tell you what will be the end of it; but He tells you one thing—that if you will be committed to Him, He will look after you, and take care of you, and He will land you at last safe in glory.

Will you be committed, my brother, my sister? Will you come and be married really and truly to the Lord Jesus this morning? Not a sham marriage, not just a ceremony. What would you think of a woman coming to the altar as a mere sham, as a mere ceremony, and then going back to live with her mother just as she did before? You would say ridiculous! and yet there are plenty of professing disciples who come and do it with Him, and go back and live as they did before. Come and be really married this morning, really committed to the interests of Jesus Christ, and be prepared to take upon you all the consequences of such a mission—this is faith.

HOPE-SO BELIEVERS.—There are two classes of people in the church, and if you go to them and ask if they are saved, they say, "I hope so." I can't find anything in the Bible on that line, that tells a man just to hope he is saved. I don't want any of those conversions. The other day I read about an evangelist who said in his meetings, "Everybody that wants to be good put your name down on this card," and then he called them saved. I believe in a man going down on his marrow bones and just crying for mercy. If we have but half a dozen people converted we are going to have it so they know it. I am sick of this slip-shod way of converting; we don't want any more of it, but what we want to get is men that know they are saved. If your religion don't keep you from thinking swear in your heart, it is no religion at all. "Are you saved?" I hope so. Hope so? What do you hope? Have you passed from death into life? Have all things been made new? Has such a change taken place in you that you don't want to swear any more? If religion don't take that all out of you it is not religion at all. What we want are genuine Holy Ghost conversions. When I go up to the Pearly Gates of Heaven I want to see them standing around the throne of God. I don't want any hope so. God deliver us from that kind. I want religion that is going to change you from the crown of your head to the sole of your feet. I want to get it so that everybody will know it; even the cat and the dog about the house. I wouldn't give a cent for a man that calls himself a Christian and beats his horse to death just because he balks; a pretty Christian he is; or a lady that abuses her servant girl, and never asks her in to prayers just because she is a servant; a pretty Christian she is, isn't she? "Are you saved?" "You hope so?" If you don't show by your actions that you love your wife, you are a mean man; there is no hope so about it. There is nothing a wife loves so well as for her husband to slip up behind her and say "Sally, I love you." Therefore, my brother and sister, hoping so won't do you any good. I hope you are all rich, but you are not. If I could make the people rich by hoping so, I would do it, but that don't bring it. Now, I hope there will be ten thousand people converted in this town, but my hoping so won't convert them. The Bible says, "We know," and if you don't know you have never been converted, God bless you. It is no farther from the church to hell than it is from the world; the distance is just the same. "Are you saved?" You talk about being saved, and then go to the theatre. A man or woman that will go to the theatre, or dance or play cards in the Methodist church is a hypocrite. You promised when you came into this church that you would not do these things, and just as sure as you do these, you are a hypocrite. They did not dance or play cards in my church. I promised the conference I would live up to the rules of the Methodist church, and if a preacher don't do it he is just as bad as the rest of them. I have been in lots of places where they say: "Mr. Weber, if I was to be converted I could not dance, and I must dance." I tell you there was never a boy this side of Heaven that enjoyed dancing as much as I did. Holy people don't dance or let their daughters dance or play cards; they don't do it. Sanctified people don't think about those things. "Are you saved?" "You hope so." "The Bible says "*We know so.*" What do you do with the Bible? Do you say, Mr. Weber, I don't understand it so. The Epistle of John has the verb "To know" forty-two times in five chapters. Why, the Bible is full of "To know." I want to say to you if you don't know what you are converted from, you never were converted. I don't want a man converted to me; I want you to be converted to God, so that when I leave this place they will find you at the class meeting; they can call on you at any moment; that is the kind of conversions we want here. We do not want any more of this slip-shod work here. "*Are you saved?*" "*You hope so.*" *That don't do. See Peter and John and James and Thaddeus and the rest of them rejoicing, and Jesus said: "What are you rejoicing for?" Because we saw the devil fall as lightning from Heaven. Do not rejoice about that, but "Rejoice that your names are written in Heaven!"*

KNOW-SO RELIGION.—Paul says "We know we have passed from death unto life." What do you know? We know we have passed from death to life. There are some of you church members who would be strange ornaments in Heaven. Say, my brothers and sisters, do you know that after the spirit of God takes hold of you it will save you. I have had men that would tonight crush me under their feet, yet I could get right down and lick up the spit from under their feet, because I love them. Hereby we do know that we know Him. Why? Because we keep His commandments. It is a thousand times more easy for you to sin than for you to do right; unless you are in the way of doing right it is hard to do right. You become a new creature in Christ Jesus, and some how or other you love to talk about Jesus. "Are you saved?" If you are not saved, my brothers and sisters, and you don't know that you are saved, you have not passed from death unto life. God says unless a man be born again he cannot enter the kingdom of Heaven. Nicodemus was a better man than you are; why, he stood in the highest official position; he lived before the world as a Christian, but what did Jesus say to him? You must be born again. Ye must be born from above; born twice and die once and go to Heaven or to be born once and die twice and go to hell. "Are you saved?" You are a member of the church, but that don't save you. Once I had a good deal of money, but I havn't it now. Once you had good health, but you have not got it now. Once you might have been a Christian, but you are not now; remember, that to be a Christian is to be Christ-like. Before you come to kneel at this altar and say put me down as converted, you have got to tell this congregation that you are saved. "Are you saved?" Yes; how do you know? Here is a little boy who has fallen in the water; I went down and pulled him out. Another man comes along and says: "Say, my boy, are you saved?" "I hope so." I tell you, the little fellow would not be that big a fool, and don't you be a big enough fool to say that. If you don't know that you are saved, don't say so till you do know, but say, "Oh, Father, convert my soul! Oh, God, take sin out of my heart and help me to be Christ-like!" And as sure as there is a God in Heaven He will.

How Much Do You Pray.—Prayer is the medium by which we get near to God. We find that men who accomplished much for God were men of much prayer.

"Enoch walked with God;" that is, he prayed continually. Jacob, when he was anxious to get the blessing, prayed all night.

After David had numbered Israel and sinned, when the destroying angel appeared to smite Jerusalem, he and the elders fell on their faces, and with sackcloth and deep humiliation persuaded God to stop the angel from destroying the city; thus prevailing in prayer.

Daniel spent twenty-one days in constant prayer to get an answer. Many of us would have given up, and got discouraged. Sometimes we must continue long in prayer, if answers are to come.

Jesus spent all night in prayer, not that He needed faith, for all faith and love was full in Him, but to set an example for us.

The Disciples spent, according to Arthur's "Tongue of Fire," ten days and nights in prayer to God before the baptism of fire came. See the results! All through the revival book (the Acts) we see the Disciples prayed much and long.

The early fathers of the church were men who prayed much.

Now and then, during the dark ages, history records monks who moved things, and lived holy, and accomplished much for God, but who spent hours in prayer daily.

Luther said: "If I fail to spend two hours in prayer each morning, the devil gets the victory during the day."

Knox said: "Give me Scotland, or I die." See the Scottish Church as the result. 'Tis said, "Mary, Queen of Scots, feared his prayers more than any army!"

Our beloved Wesley was a mighty man of prayer, and always spent an hour or two each day for wisdom and power to lead men and women to God.

Whitfield lived in the atmosphere of prayer. See how the thousands were converted under his ministry!

Fletcher killed himself fasting and praying. Not many of us will die that way!

Bramwell would not be in a town a fortnight before the whole town would be aroused religiously, and hundreds would be saved.

Billy Bray smote the hosts of sin in his peculiar way, because he was a man who lived and walked with God. Oh, what a man of prayer he was!

Finney, the prince of evangelists, prayed much, and carried a man with him who would pray while he was preaching. When we get to glory we'll see the tens of thousands he led to God.

Edwards and his faithful band prayed all night, and the next day the convicting Spirit of God so manifested himself, that the elders threw their arms around the pillars of the church, and cried: "Lord, save me, I'm slipping down to hell!"

Payson wore the hard wood boards into grooves where his knees had pressed so often and long. Read his life, and see what were the scenes around the altars of his church.

Take every man or woman who has been a great blessing in the hands of God, and turned many to righteousness, and you will find they were those who spent hours in prayer.

Brother and Sister, how much do you pray? Is it your chief delight? Are you the happiest when you are face to face with God? Do you at all times flee to God in prayer when temptation, trial, or disappointment comes?

Minister, chosen of God, do you pray an hour or two each day for the baptism of the Holy Ghost to come on you and the people? Are you living so God can use you to win others for Jesus? Is your chief aim to please the people, or God? Are you sure you are wholly His, perfectly consecrated to His work, and the greatest desire of your heart to see souls saved, and Christians sanctified? If you can answer in the affirmative, you can depend on it that you will see the desires of your heart. Father, in Jesus' name, give us pure hearts, and make us like Jesus. Amen!

ADVANTAGES OF PRAYER.—Prayer can obtain everything. It can open the windows of Heaven, and shut the gates of hell. It can put a holy constraint upon

God, and detain an angel till he leave a blessing. It can open the treasures of rain, and soften the iron ribs of rocks till they melt into tears and a flowing river. Prayer can unclasp the girdle of the North, saying to a mountain of ice, be thou removed hence and cast into the bottom of the sea. It can arrest the sun in the midst of his course, and send the swift-winged wind upon our errand, and all those strange things, and secret decrees and unrevealed transactions, which are above the clouds and far beyond the regions of the stars, shall combine in ministry and advantages for the praying man.

COUNSELS TO THE SAINTS.—1. From a valued correspondent, an evangelist of experience, observation, prudence and wisdom, who travels far and wide, we have the following:

"Enclosed you will find a letter containing a question which is often asked of me by different persons.

" In this case I replied:

" *Make sure of your own experience first.*

" *Then keep sweet.*

" *Be true to the church.*

" *Never go back on your testimony; but let it be given in the spirit of Christ.*

Be careful to avoid even the appearance of an attempt to antagonize your pastor.

" *Yet, at the same time, be careful to avoid compromise, etc.*

" I thought, perhaps, the Lord would give you something good to give such inquirers through the *Standard*. These are not easy questions for one like myself to answer and they come often.

"Is it not hard to conceive of such a Methodist preacher? Yet in our state there are many such."

2. We append the question above referred to, and a few sentences from the letter containing it.

"Permit a stranger to inquire of you what a member of our church is to do who wishes to enjoy the blessing of holiness where the preacher neither teaches or believes in it?

"I am taking the *Christian Standard*, which teaches this doctrine. One year ago last summer I attended camp-meeting at Decatur. I had the pleasure of hearing Brothers Smith and Pepper. Since that time my mind has been occupied more or less with this subject."

3. We think the answers given by our correspondent to this inquirer could hardly be made clearer or better.

In addition to what she wrote, we always feel like urging the few holiness people who find but little sympathy from pastors or fellow members?

1. To have some convenient place of meeting. Perhaps the best place for them to meet would be in a private house.

2. Never let these meetings conflict with any of the regular services of the church.

3. Don't bother the preacher to announce them. Quietly secure the attendance of others by personal invitation.

4. *Don't be discouraged if many do not come.*
5. *Converse on the deep things of God.*
6. *Tell one another your experiences of perfect love.*
7. Have a holiness circulating library.
8. Introduce a good holiness paper. Get it into as many homes as you can.
9. Read to one another in your meetings extracts from the paper and from holiness books.
10. *Work constantly, sweetly, patiently, lovingly, gently, to get others entirely sanctified.*
11. Have a holy independence of character, conversation, experience, life, and work.

THE MINISTRY OF STEPHEN.—How unable are the world and a degenerate ecclesiasticism to resist the wisdom and spirit of a seraphic Stephen, whose honest report, whose wisdom, whose fulness of faith and of the Holy Ghost, whose pentecostal power, have filled his soul with fire, his lips with arguments, his face with heavenly glory, his speech with convincing energy.

Not that they will yield willingly to these; not that they will give up their errors; not that they will cease their active opposition to the truth. While Stephen is yet speaking, and doing great wonders and miracles among the people, they are at their old, old business of disputing; of suborning men to bear false witness against him, to charge him with blasphemy against Moses, against "this holy place," against the law, against God; of stirring up the people and the elders and scribes to come upon him, to catch him, to bring him to the council; of securing testimony that he is saying that Jesus of Nazareth will destroy this place, and change the customs which Moses delivered us.

It is the time-worn conflict between true spirituality and formal religion; between Christianity and church-ianity; between rites and customs, antecedents and traditions, establishments and authority, and the fulness of faith and of the Holy Ghost.

Nevertheless, the divinely given wisdom and spirit of Stephen are resistless. They sweep on to the very gates of heaven. They light up his face with angelic rapture. They leave a testimony that rises out of the very ashes of the fire that consumes them. They are a perpetual arraignment of consciences, customs and conduct. They crumble ecclesiasticism into the dust. They build real Christianity as by magic upon the ruins of a powerful and proud but degenerate formalism. Stephen may be stoned; his Lord may receive his spirit; he may disappear from earthly circles; but his spirit and his wisdom remain in resistless force till the final consummation.

In our measure we may be his successors. We may drink in a double portion of his spirit. We may have the same, perhaps even greater wisdom from on high. The same resistless eloquence and logic or fire may fall from lips of heavenly flame. Angelic glory may shine out of our faces. Martyrdom may carry us to the bosom of God, to the presence of Christ, to the company of heaven, to joys immortal. Be our ministry long or short, peaceful or troubled, popular or unpopular, let us be sure that Stephen's spirit and wisdom are in it.

"———— *is a hard place for holiness.*" So is every place. *Don't be discouraged. Don't allow yourself to say or think such things. Look above all second causes to the First Great Cause. God can make any place soft for holiness, if He chooses, and if you don't stop Him by your unbelief, and by talking about "hard places." That is only one form of talking out our unbelief. Pray on, believe on, march on, work on, hope ever, look on the cheery side, "never say die."*

There are Methodist **parents** who allow their children to grow up dancers, card-players and theater-goers, and then are surprised that the children drift away from the Methodist church. But they will not unite with a church which condemns their favorite amusements.

WASH-TUB CONSECRATED.—You who are doing nothing for God, because you "have not the ability," read this:

Amanda Smith was born a slave. Freed by the war, she worked as a washerwoman in New York. In a meeting led by Mr. Inskip she received Christ as her Sanctifier. After speaking in meetings for some time with much fruit, the question came from the Lord as to whether she would go wholly into the work of preaching and trust him for her support. I have heard her tell (in India) of the struggle she had over this call. At last she "laid her wash-tub and flat-iron on the altar," as she expressed it, and went out to preach, "looking unto Jesus."

At a camp-meeting near Bombay I heard her urge God's children to accept the riches of full salvation. She brought up the old objection of counterfeit humility that "holiness is too high a blessing for those who have been so down in sin as we," and dealt with it this way: "Now, s'pose some one had given me ten thousand lacs of rupees—I don't know how much that is, but I s'pose it's a good deal"—[about $400,000,000!] "and s'pose I was drivin' along that grand street in Bombay among the big folks in my great carriage," (and her tall form, reminding you of the Queen of Sheba!) "and then some one should holler out: 'There goes 'Mandy Smith; I knew her when she was doin' washin' for her livin'!' What dy'e think I'd do? (Earnest pause). I'd drive on! I'D DRIVE ON!! I'D DRIVE ON!!!" This was uttered in the rising emphasis of truly impassioned oratory, and the application was most powerful—begging every soul to claim all God's salvation gives, driving right on in spite of all the criticism of the "accuser of the brethren" and his human agents.

SEED-THOUGHTS FOR SOUL-SAVERS.—Soul-saving is here considered as a human work. "He which converteth the sinner from the error of his way shall save a soul from death, and shall hide a multitude of sins." In its broader sense it embraces the turning of souls from sin, pointing them to Christ, training them for God and leading them to Heaven.

Christian life at its best is the perpetuation of the Christ life. "The Son of man came to seek and to save that which was lost." Jesus soon vanished from earth, leaving the work of winning souls from sin to His followers. If we do it not, as Christ would do if in our place, we have not the Spirit of Christ, and are none of His. Every Christian is a commissioned soul-saver. We are called to catch men. To deny the obligation or to evade the task, is to disown our Master, or shirk our calling.

Angels are plenty, and God could send droves of them to warn men and woo them to righteousness; but that would cheat us of sharing in the sweets and glory of redeeming the world. I know we are "called to be saints." Our first call is unto holiness. But a holiness that does not duplicate the zeal of the soul-seeking Savior lacks the genuine stamp and seal.

"Ye," not angels, "are the light of the world." Jesus could not get to Nathanael except through Philip. Is life worth living? Yes, the Christ-life is. If it paid Jesus to live in the flesh, it will pay you. But there is nothing to offset the drudgery and toil of life on the earth but the glory of seeking, saving and serving the lost.

Have you considered that Heaven is watching us and is dependent somewhat for its joy on our efforts? "There is joy in Heaven over one sinner that repenteth. All earth's news that they are reported as caring to learn about up yonder is the salvation of souls. Every effort to win a soul stirs fresh life all through the celestial city. What are you doing to make Jesus glad and angels jubilant?

Centuries ago the harvest was great and the "laborers few." How much more so now! When the storm is approaching, how lively the harvesters toil to garner sheaves against destruction and loss! What harvest owner will dally or trifle when the crop is dead ripe and crying, "Come and save me?" But the call of earthly business is child's play compared with the Father's business of redeeming a sin-cursed world. Men of the world push and boom their affairs; but who is urging on the Savior's work? He is crying, "Go ye." "Why stand ye idle?" "The night cometh." Hurry up, lest some starving Lazarus perish at the door, through sheer neglect.

"The soul that watereth shall himself be watered." A conservative holiness will soon grow tame and tasteless. There is no employment so exhilarating as working with Jesus in saving the lost. Angels would pay a large premium to exchange opportunities with the Christians on earth. Yet how many good "professors" of religion are all but sleeping while their companions slumber with no oil in their vessels! Paul might well return and cry, "Awake to righteousness, and sin not; for some have not the knowledge of God; I speak this to your shame." The brilliant experiences are the property of incessant soul-winners.

The awards of the Judgment will reveal the full importance of winning souls on earth. "They that be wise shall shine as the brightness of the firmament, and they that turn many to righteousness, as the stars forever and ever." Talk about "star preachers" and "star performers." The "star" saints are those who turn many to Jesus. Treasure in Heaven is the record of much fruit on earth. What are your deposits? Heaven's millionaires will be found among those who "ceased not to warn every one night and day with tears," who "were made all things to all men," that they "might by all means save some." Even our resurrection bodies shall vary in honor growing out of our "labor in the Lord," which is "not in vain."

When God shall muster into rank His heroes in the "great day," mere body rescuers, fame finders, fact gatherers, adventurers, and even philanthropists and reformers will take their place in the rear of soul-winners. This is not written to disparage other than specific religious work, but to stimulate a special line of Christian duty possible to all. Every saint may be, and must be a practical soul-winner, or forfeit much glory from his crown. If he follows up his new-born instincts, the converted man will find his life-business. Led on and sanctified by the Holy Ghost, he will find his passion for souls quickening. Alas! that in so many, fear or passion has quenched this burning ambition of God in the soul! Is it so with you? Are you an active and reputed soul-saver? Can the Master call you one of His successful, skillful and untiring harvest-hands? If so, or otherwise, you will find profit in following these brief Seed-Thought papers.

How to Have a Revival.—1st. Get revived yourself. Get your soul on fire. Consecrate all to God. Let Him make you perfect in love.

2d. Remember that time is short. Eternity near. That you, your parents, children, brother, sister, friends, neighbors, all mankind, are on their way to heaven or hell. That all are near, and some on the brink of eternity, and soon it will be too late to save them.

3d. Begin *now*. Pray for a revival. Pray on.

Keep praying. Pray till you die.

Work for a revival. Work on. Keep working. Work till you die.

Trust. Trust on. Keep trusting. Trust till you die.

Try this expedient. Try that. Try the other. Keep trying. Try till you die.

That's the way you cleared your farm.

That's the way you built your house.

That's the way you got your education.

That's the way you made your money.

That's the way you got all that's worth having.

That's the way to have a revival.

CHILDREN AND REVIVALS.—Every genuine revival seeks the salvation of the children. They are usually the easiest reached and make the most substantial workers in the church.

It is estimated that over three-fourths of the people who are saved were converted before they were twenty years of age.

Children often are among the most effective workers in revival meetings. "A little child shall lead them," has proved true of many adults who have been led to the altar through the influence of some precious child.

We were once in a revival where many children were converted. Some said, "Nobody but children," but in a few years these very children were the leading spirits in that community. God bless the children!

HOW NOT TO HAVE A REVIVAL.—Don't pray for it. Don't believe for it.

Look at the obstacles and consider them insurmountable.

Conclude that yours is a very wicked place.

That there is a great deal of skepticism.

That the people are "Gospel hardened."

That the church is too cold and dead.

That it is too weak and has too little social standing.

That the preacher isn't much of a revivalist anyhow.

That there are too few workers.

That there is too much else going on.

That the weather is unfavorable.

Hatch up any one or more of a thousand such excuses.
Or, make a little spasmodic half-hearted effort.
Expect to fail and do it.
Or, put all other lines of church work first.
Give all the time to them.
Don't try to have a revival.

In that way you won't be troubled with one and you will have the satisfaction of seeing your church grow beautifully less from year to year and your children, friends and neighbors go down to hell.

THE SHORT CUT TO A REVIVAL.—*Any church this side of perdition can have a revival.* "When?" *Before to-morrow's sun shall set.* "How?" *By calling in the greatest and only Revivalist.* "Where does he live?" *Not far from any one of us.* "What is his name?" *The Holy Spirit.* "But must not the church first get right?" *No. He will come to make the church right. A small committee with God can chase a thousand,* and put in flames with tongues of fire a heap of rubbish. If all the Achans, in all the churches, had to be put without the camp before God could send a pentecostal outpouring, the Israel of to-day might well hang her harps on the willows and despair of the millennium ever coming. Heat will melt ice, and a revival will cure chills. Smoke will drive chipmunks out of their holes, but it will take a Heaven-kindled fire to drive a cold professor to the altar of prayer, or out of the church. There are not a few churches in which a pentecost would be considered a catastrophe. These churches might safely pull down their lightning rods. The fire that such edifices are at present in danger of is not from above. And yet in an ecclesiastical ice house children may be born. The births at first will be very quiet, and it may be necessary to hurry the little ones into a warmer clime to prevent them catching a fatal chill. Better to be born at a spiritual North Pole than to die forever. A mourner's bench and few converts will do much to arouse a dead church. Once started, the revival contagion will spread. The converts may chill, but the church will warm. Once in, the leaven will lift. The faint-hearted will rally. Success will succeed. Lines will be drawn. Forces will meet. When the Spartan force is found who will win or die, the victory will be sure.

FAITH FOR REVIVAL RESULTS.—Expect a Revival. "Ask God and believe Him." Be as persistent and confident of final victory as was a Christian woman who wished to get a school house in which to hold a Sabbath School. The trustee was skeptical and refused to give her the key.

Still she persevered, and entreated him again and again. "I tell you, Aunt Polly, it is of no use. Once for all, you cannot have the school house for any such purpose." "I think I am going to get it," said Aunt Polly. "I should like to know how, if I do not give you the key?" "I think the Lord is going to unlock it." "Maybe He will," said the infidel, "but I can tell you

this, that He is not going to get the key away from me."
"Well, I am going to pray over it, and I have found
out from experience that when I keep on praying, *something must give way*," and the next time she came the
hard heart of the infidel gave way, and she received the
key.

Of course the devil will rage and seek to stop the Revival. But what if he does? Has not Christ promised
to give "power over all the power of the enemy?" Then
vanquish him in Jesus' name and by His power.

The greater the obstacle to a Revival the more urgent
the need of it. It is when the "enemy comes in like a
FLOOD" that God expressly agrees to "lift up a standard
against him."

HOME HINTS—THE EDUCATING POWER OF EXAMPLE.—Household life is ever giving the children its
unconscious training. It is not so much what we say to
the child, as what we say and do in its presence, that has
a formative influence upon its character.

Ruskin, in speaking of his childhood, says: "I never
had heard my father's or mother's voice once raised in
any question with each other; nor seen an angry, or
even slightly hurt or offended glance in the eyes of
either. I had never heard a servant scolded; nor even
suddenly, passionately, or in any severe manner, blamed.
I had never seen a moment's trouble or disorder in any
household matter; nor anything whatever either done
in a hurry or undone in due time. . . . Nothing was

ever promised me that was not given; nothing ever threatened me that was not inflicted, and nothing ever told me that was not true."

Can we wonder that, as the result of this, Ruskin could say: "I obeyed word or lifted finger of father or mother simply as a ship her helm; not only without idea of resistance, but receiving the direction as a part of my own life and force, a helpful law, as necessary to me in every moral action as the law of gravity in leaping."

Such training as this, both in precept and example, is rare, very rare; if tempered by love, it would seem almost perfect.

We should expect to find noble men and women in families thus reared. They breathe in a constant atmosphere of faith and obedience, and like healthy plants raised in congenial soil, they are developed to the highest possibility of their attainment.

But what of children reared in an impoverished soil in which no virtues can thrive, and the good seed, chance-sown, is parched, and finds no nutrition? Those in industrial schools, in missions of various kinds, in the tenement house and the cellar, how can love and faith, obedience, and a knowledge of our duty to God and man, find growth and development? But even in better homes we sometimes find formal instruction given in studied phrases, while the reverse is taught by the daily habits of the household. Perhaps the positive evil in such cases is worse than the sins of neglect resulting from the ignorance of the lower class. The child from the tenement house may, perhaps, listen to the story of God's love to us, and be touched by it, because suffering and want may have opened its heart to the need of Christ, the great Burden-bearer. But where the child as yet has had no suffering, and comparatively no wants, it has never felt the need of a Saviour's love, and it is not attracted by the very formal presentation of love and duty which at stated times is placed before it.

The story is told of that well-known wall motto, "God bless our home," being used as a missile between a quarreling pair.

We are almost inclined to smile at the contrast between the words and the act, but it is, after all, only a coarse picture of the antagonism between the spoken words and the actual life in merely nominal Christian families. And what is the effect upon the children? As, according to the old adage, actions speak louder than words, the child is educated under the more emphatic instruction of what it sees.

There are parents who, because they are in good social position themselves, are unwilling to believe that their children are guilty of what they are pleased to consider the sins of low life. "Of course, my children would never lie nor steal," says the thoughtless, complacent mother. She does not give them the instruction which might guard them against such sins, and she even resents the insinuation that it is needed in the Sunday-school. Nevertheless, she is teaching them daily by her example and her unguarded words.

A group of children were together at play. A bright, shrewd little girl was personating mamma receiving calls. In a corner which was supposed to represent mamma's dressing-room, the child is handed by one of her playmates what is supposed to be the card of a visitor in the parlor. The little girl frowns. She scowls in exact and clever mimicry of anger and dislike as she exclaims: "Oh, I can't bear that woman, the silly creature!" She stamps her little foot as if on the neck of an enemy. Then she runs into the suppositious parlor, exclaiming in tones of rapturous and joyful greeting: "My dear Mrs. Smith! Delighted to see you! How kind of you to come!" etc. This is not a fancy sketch. It was an actual occurrence.

A little lad was congratulated by a young companion on the possession of a good ball. Where did you get it? was the not unnatural inquiry.

"Fred and I were playing together. He bounced it so hard that we could not find it. But after he went home I found it in a hole. I'll keep it. He has so many balls he can spare this one." Not a word about returning it. The mother at the piazza window overhears the conversation, and, laughing, says to papa: "Let Joe alone for getting what he wants!"

When Joe grows to be a man, he may help himself to the property of others in a way that causes the mother's heart to ache. But by that time she will have forgotten how early he began that course of appropriating to himself that which rightfully belonged to another.

Thus it happens oftentimes that what we fail to say has its effect, and the silence that gives consent has its educating power as well as the words that are spoken. The example set before us is so much easier to follow than the mere direction.

The guide stood beside the Mer de Glace. "How shall I cross it?" asked the traveler. The guide replied, but the words were in a foreign tongue.

"Follow in his footsteps," said one beside the traveler. No farther instruction was needed.

Paul, in his directions for life and doctrine to Titus, whom he calls "mine own son after the faith," while bidding him exhort young men, adds, "In all things showing thyself a pattern of good works."

May we not accept the order of the Apostle's teaching, and while we exhort the young, also add that other and more potent form of instruction—that of being ourselves the pattern and example of what we teach.

A SAMPLE OF THE TRACTS HE USED—THESE SEEM TO BE ORIGINAL.

ACCIDENTS.

LOST:—

At the theatre the other night, my Christian experience.—*Presumptuous Professor.*

BADLY HURT:—

My soul, at a progressive euchre party, that one of our fashionable sisters persuaded me to attend. Pray for me.—*A Penitent Sister.*

POISONED.

Miss Unwilling-to-be-Advised was found so badly affected by a dime novel last Sabbath that she could not attend the afternoon meeting.

FOUND FROZEN TO DEATH!

A prominent church member, who began wandering from the regular weekly meeting, next attended the show, then the horse race, afterwards went fishing on the Sabbath, and was finally found stone dead, spiritually, in the grocery store, listening to prurient stories and blasphemy against Christianity.—*Life Boat.*

BIBLE READING.

UNBELIEF AND ITS RESULTS.

UNBELIEF weakens Christians and renders them unfit for the work of God.—Matt. xvii: 14-20.

UNBELIEF prevents Christians from receiving the fullness of God's blessing.—Heb. iii: 17-19.

UNBELIEF produces spiritual shipwreck.—Rom. xi: 20-22.

Christians warned ESPECIALLY against UNBELIEF.—Heb. iii: 7-12.

Zacharias, a priest of God, was punished for his unbelief in a very marked manner.—Luke i: 18-20.

Christ can do no great work where there is unbelief. —Mark vi: 5-6.

FOOT NOTES.

Are you, by unbelief, retarding the success of these meetings?

In which have you most faith, God's power to SAVE or the institutions of evil to wreck?

You can, by unbelief, as effectually stay the baptism of God's Spirit as by a positive refusal to work. (Without FAITH it is impossible to please God.—Heb. x: 1-6.)

"All things are possible to him that believeth."

STARTLING FOR FALSE PROFESSORS.

Not every one that saith unto me, Lord, Lord, shall enter into the Kingdom of Heaven, but he that doeth the will of my Father who is in Heaven.—Matt. 7: 21.

THE EXPERIENCE OF A PRESIDING ELDER ON HOLINESS.—On account of the contents of this letter, I am very glad I have not given you my full name. Those who read my account of the "holiness convention," at Gainesville, Northeast Georgia, doubtless observed that I did not express an opinion as to the propriety or impropriety of such a meeting, or as to the genuineness or spuriousness of the experiences given at that meeting. Now that nearly a week has passed since that meeting, I wish to say that after having attended revival meetings for twenty-six years, I never was in a meeting where there was so much of the constant presence and power of the Holy Ghost. At that meeting I think at least thirty, perhaps forty, persons testified to having been sanctified and obtained perfect love. Experience may not be taken as the highest evidence, but experience cannot be gainsaid. The Lord said, "Ye are my witnesses."

I have nothing to say now as to the different theories on the subject, but I must say that I will be glad and rejoice the remainder of my days, that I went to that holiness meeting at Gainesville, Ga. I knew who the leaders in the meeting would be, and though I loved these brethren—Dunlap, Dodge, Patillo, Butler, Jarrell, Timmons, (B. E. L.) Reese, Willis and others—yet I was not in full sympathy with their professions of instantaneous sanctification. I was in the city of Atlanta and debated for two hours whether to go to the meeting, fifty miles away, northeast from Atlanta, or to go home, having been absent from my family for weeks. I hardly think I decided the question at all, but I found myself on the Gainesville-bound train. The first testimonies given as to salvation from all sin—inbred sin, and as to the obtaining of perfect love, rather grated on my ears. However, I wondered why I should be offended at a profession of holiness by others, which I and every Methodist preacher preaches. I soon found that the preachers, laymen and women, who professed what they called "the blessing of perfect love," had something I had never obtained. They all told the same story, showed the same humility, and they all alike magnified the Lord Jesus and the atoning blood, and all alike showed an absolute want of fear or timidity. I talked, too, a little in a general way; I said that I was upon God's altar;

that I was consecrated in heart and life to God and His service; that I was willing to lay down my life, if necessary, for the sake of Christ Jesus and His gospel; nevtheless I had a burdened heart. The burden grew heavier by the hour. I prayed almost incessantly for two days and nights. I slept during these two nights but an hour or so at a time. My last thoughts before sleeping and the first in waking were prayer. I propounded to myself these questions, with many others: Did I not give my heart to God when but a boy? Have I not been in the enjoyment of religion nearly all my life? Was I not very happy only a week ago? Have I committed sin since that time? Have I not had the witness of the Spirit for days past? Why, then, this burden of heart? Why this deep distress and almost unbearable agony of soul? My prayer was: Lord, search me to the deepest depths of my heart;

> "Turn each cursed idol out
> That dares to rival Thee."

It was brought to my recollection that I had always loved to hear my sermons praised by others, which now seemed to be human pride. And I remembered that at times I dreamed of wealth and worldly ease, and this seemed to savor of covetousness. Anyhow, I concluded my heart had not been entirely cleansed from moral pollution. I began to pray for the cleansing of the blood of Christ, and I reached the point where I was willing for God to take all inbred sin out of my heart. But this temptation came. I suppose it was the tempter said to me: "Are you going to join the holiness people? It will be a nice spectacle for you to rise up before a congregation and say you are sanctified. The people will say you are gone crazy on religion." But I at last reached the point where I was willing "to bear the reproach of Christ, to be the filth and offscouring of the world; and looking that men should say all manner of evil * * falsely for the Lord's sake." But I fully realized that I was wanting in faith. It seemed I could not believe that God would do this great work for me. On all sides these holiness brethren and sisters said: "Believe! believe! It is all by faith." I was trying to believe. I was more than humiliated at the thought that though I had preached more than a hundred times on faith, and explained faith to hundreds of people, and, as I thought, made the subject plain, now that I was trying to believe that God would cleanse my heart, it seemed that I knew nothing at all about faith. I finally realized that I was in a transition state, but from what, and to what, I did not know. The holiness meeting commenced Monday; on Friday morning I began to realize a sweet and abiding peace. The Lord Jesus seemed to be very near to me and very precious. At the close of the meeting, on Friday, at which there was great power of the Spirit, I stated publicly that I had received a peace that was abiding, and a baptism of the Spirit I had never had—that they might call it a second or third or hundredth blessing—I did not care what they called it—but I had received a work of grace in my heart never before enjoyed. After retiring to my room that night, a flood-tide of love and peace came into my heart. It was with some difficulty I restrained shouts of joy at the hour of midnight. On Saturday morning I left for my work, and preached Saturday morning and night, and also Sunday morning and night. That Sunday was the happiest day of my life. I had a constant baptism of the Spirit—had a discernment of the moral state of men I never had before, and a boldness in proclaiming gospel truth for which I had long prayed. Four days have passed since the blessing was first manifested in my heart, and my peace and faith in the blessed Christ is still the same. I feel that I am less than the least and Jesus greater than the greatest. I never had so low an estimation of myself—never had so high, or rather such strong and abiding faith in the Lord Jesus. Call me specialist, hobbyist, sanctificationist, or what you choose, the language of my heart constantly is, "The blood cleanseth! the blood cleanseth! blessed be the name of the Lord forever!" As I rode on the train yesterday, I wanted to talk to every one I knew, and even those with whom I had no acquaintance, about the cleansing blood. Reader, has your heart been cleansed from all sin? Have you perfect love—love without a mixture of hatred; faith without any mixture of doubt; peace that is abiding and not fluctuating? And when you seek this blessing, remember that it is a great calm and not a storm.

ASBURY.

ORIGINAL MATTER.

It is said of Napoleon the First that he inquired of one of his artisans if he could make a bullet-proof armor; he said, "yes." When he had made it the General said, "Now, put it on;" which was done. The General took his pistol and fired again and again, but it stood fire and was approved. Now, can we go forth and defy the world, the flesh and the devil? because we have on the whole armor of God, we are wrapped up in the 13th of 1st Cor.

Shall the XIth of Hebrews be wings or weights? Out of weakness were made strong, just by taking God at His word, or *using* that much misunderstood word, faith.

In the XII chapter we have just the opposite of XIth, that which binds the hands of Omnipotence, for He could not do many mighty works because of their unbelief, and it brought to mind an incident told by a Brother Jacques: He used to go to a shady place to prepare his sermons, when he noticed a bug go up nineteen times, go up a precipice and fall back every time. Weary with its failures, it stretched out its wings and mounted up like an eagle over the place.

Here lies one of the grand Ocean steamers. Now go aboard of her, walk into the splendid cabin, all the sofas of plush and velvet, and cushioned chairs; go next and look at the splendid engine; and now fifteen feet under the water are the furnaces; here is an engine of 3,000 horse-power, and not a move; why? they have no steam to run her with; brass all polished, machinery all in order; now fire her up and let the steam come, and away she moves like a thing of life.

The wheat in the hands of the Egyptian mummy remained thousands of years, but when put into the ground brought forth an abundant harvest. We must die to all below, and set our affections on things above, then we shall have a harvest of souls.

A young man in Birmingham, Ala., from New York, just about to marry, fell into temptation and got drunk. He was published in the papers, and on hearing it gave way to depression, then destroyed himself. Psalm ix:17.

Psalm xv. and 2nd verse: "And speaketh the truth in his heart."

MILLEDGEVILLE, Nov. 5th, 1886.

A young man from ——— carried his intended bride to church; the collectors came round and the young man showed a five dollor gold piece to her; she thought that was too much for him to give; he told her he often did that in a strange church. He slipped the gold piece in his pocket and gave a quarter; the collection was counted and amounted to $3.75. Annanias and Sapphira did little more than this, for God looketh at the heart. What do you intend to do by giving that money? Is it to please God? then you speak the truth rather than act the truth. The young sister broke up the match and that was her cause. Acts v and 2nd.

Matthew xxv and 34th: "Come ye blessed;" "Depart ye cursed," Matthew xxv: 41. A million dollars a word is said to be the price of a sentence of the presiding judge of the Supreme Court of Pennsylvania October 18th. The judge pronounced the decision in eleven words. He said: "Decree affirmed, and appeal dismissed at the cost of the appellants." Eleven millions of dollars determined the ownership of in those few words. What costly words, you say; but there are a few more costly words than these, and they are spoken by the Judge of all the earth, and decides the ownership of Heaven or Hell, and they are: "Come, ye blessed of my Father, inherit the kingdom prepared for you from the foundation of the world," or "depart, ye cursed, into everlasting fire prepared for the Devil and his angels."

Dearly Beloved Brother Dodge:

"Except a corn of wheat fall into the ground and die, it abideth alone," John xii: 24. This is what Brother and Sister Smith and I profess to be doing. Dying to the world and its applause. For the glory of God, we want to write this letter. We left Waycross for Homerville, Ga., on Saturday, October 19th. The Lord was with us there in power, Luke xxi: 49. Many bright conversions and clear sanctifications, 1st Thess. 5: 23. We arrived in Hilliard, Fla., October 25th. The Spirit of God still deigns to use us, and souls are being saved in Florida. All glory to our God! We ask all readers of the "*Way of Life*" to pray for us, that God will keep us in the dust, and that He will put the "S. S." on our names—"Soul Savers." Your less than the least brother, 1st Thess. 5 and 23, S. MILLER WILLIS.

CHAPTER XIV.

MILLER WILLIS—BY REV. R. W. BIGHAM, OF THE NORTH GA. CONFERENCE.

Miller Willis was a religious prodigy. He was of an excellent family, Augusta, Georgia. Weird as John the Baptist, irrepressible as St. Paul, only a layman, I suppose in his strange life he was immediately instrumental in the conversion of not fewer than five thousand souls in Georgia, South Carolina and Florida. His converts were of all classes—in city, in country, in proudest homes, in lowliest. A great company of believers and unbelievers rise up and call him blessed.

His mother was a Christian of best qualities whose memory he nearly adored. He was of chunky build, complexion fair, black hair and eyes, body rather broad and long for his lower limbs which were set to it, and used by him awkwardly. He was a bad boy—fight quick, not counting the odds against him, hard to handle. Will resolute, free as a waterfall leaping from a peak; after conversion, gentle as peace, tender, yet true to convictions at any hazard, brave as love.

He was singularly endowed mentally. He thought quick, in a lump, reached conclusions and formed them into deeds before the average man grappled the question, or ceased wondering what he meant, or would think and do next. The business niches in his brain were mostly sealed, but he could have made a premium printer. As editor he would have put things strong, to be fought over from sunrise till death, for usually public affairs and men cannot tolerate the man that lips or prints the whole truth, especially in capitals as Miller would have done. He fought through the war—a soldierly youth worthy the Southern banner—vowed if God would spare him to get back home he would seek religion, join the church, be a faithful Christian.

He got home safely after all the battles, went again into his usual deviltries; one night in passing St. John's church while Rev. G. G. N. McDonell was preaching, he peered in at the door, went in, looked around, when his ear caught the subject, "Pay thy Vows," listened, concluded some one had crammed the preacher with him and his ways for the occasion, got mad, pressed to the preacher at the altar when service closed, and said: "Look here! I want to know who's been telling you things on me—who has been talking about me to you telling all I ever did! I demand his name."

"No one," McDonell replied, "no one."

"But somebody has," said Miller, "and you must give me his name. Folks shall not go round talking about me as if I was the worst man in Augusta, and they no better than I am."

"I don't know you," said the preacher, "have never heard of you—no one has ever mentioned you to me."

Miller turned away muttering "that's strange; a

strange preacher comes here and talks about me all through his sermon, telling the people right out in the pulpit all about my evil ways, and nobody has told him —he don't know me, never heard of me!"

He walked out under the liveoaks, angry, startled, bewildered. Concluding that the preaching was a message from God specially to him that he dare not defy, he began to pray night and day alone and wherever he heard of a prayer-meeting in the city. He was converted about seven months after the strange preacher's sermon on vows which had shown him himself. To use a phrase of Bishop Pierce—his was "a sky-blue conversion." He was revolutionized; Miller the devil, became Miller the saint, the lion was now the lamb. His life henceforth was heavenly. Had he been a Catholic he would have been canonized. As he was a Methodist his name is a household word wherever known, carrying with it the very pathos of blessing.

In telling of him in these papers, I yield to the Holy Spirit's motion, and leave the incidents to impart their own lessons, promising that, like pictures, they teach most to those who let thought have its perfect work as they read—there is much between the lines.

The first Methodist I met in Augusta, when I was presiding elder there, was Miller. While the Secretary of the Young Men's Christian Association, Rev. Marshall Lane, was trying to direct me to Prof. Derry's, now in the Wesleyan Female College, he said, "but yonder comes Miller Willis! you are all right now; he'll show you the way with all his heart." And so he did. I noticed then that he carried his Bible, as constantly as afterward, and quoted verses as we chatted on the way.

From that time till he went to Heaven from the Spartanburg home of Mr. Adams, whom I never knew but of whom Miller often spoke the best things in his own sententitious, sincere way; he loved me, prayed for, and *fussed* at me in *his* way because I couldn't understand sanctification just right. But all the same when troubles pressed him sorest, or brethren criticized him intolerantly, he would come to me or write to me.

Men on sight, or slight acquaintance, were given to calling him crazy, but he was as I have said above—after conversion, at any rate, having little or no "business sense," but he was wise to save a multitude of sinners from death, and move believers to "a closer walk with God." He knew much of the Bible by heart, nor was he a man of one book; he read many choice religious books and papers, composed, published and circulated many aptest Christian tracts. No man can read the notes in his own dear crumpled handwriting, on texts, in his Bible, or observe paragraphs he had penciled in books and papers, but knew the unique man was wise, not crazy—or crazy it was for our sakes and unto Christ—like the Christ.

I said to him one day, "Miller, take a round on the district with me." His bright eye dashed into mine, and in the moment's pause he said: "If it's the Lord's will I would like to. I've got no money to travel on, but that is nothing if He wants me to go."

"No," said I, "that's all right, we'll trust God for that. Meet me at ———. Be sure! Come." And leaving with a friend a railway ticket for him, he met me at the appointed place. He had preceded me a day, and, as his wont was, had gone through the streets exhorting all he met to be converted, or to *know* they had religion—"*know* so religion—not hope so," he phrased it. He said to a noted citizen, a backslider, but he knew it not, "have you ever been converted? Verily I say unto you except ye be converted * * ye shall not enter into the kingdom of heaven!" The citizen replied evasively. He repeated the question, adding, "make haste, delay not, escape for thy life." The gentleman cursed him and said, "You go back to Augusta; we wish none of your sort here. We have preachers of our own, good men that suit us. Go." "Never mind that," said Miller, lifting his hand toward heaven, "I am no preacher, just a layman—less than the least—but except ye be converted, and become as little children, ye cannot enter the kingdom of heaven. Turn to the Lord now, *now*." Said the citizen with oaths, "If you open your lips to me again I shall slap you over." "Then," said Miller, "I have but one thing more to say to you; *that* I will say: 'He that being often reproved, hardeneth his neck, shall suddenly be destroyed, and that without remedy;'" and passed on amid showering anathemas to persuade others. A day or two after, some ladies up the street shrieked, gentlemen whirled to the sound, the citizen was falling from his horse; they rushed to him, he was insensible and died so in a day or two.

Miller said to me one day before we left for another place, "Mr. Blank cursed me to-day." "Cursed you?" I queried. "Yes," he said, "me." I said, "Miller, he seems to be a gentleman, is so regarded here, has been mayor. Did he curse you or just curse around generally —curse at you?"

"He cursed *me* good," he replied. "You never knew a little fellow to get a plainer cursing out than he gave me. I had talked to him about his soul before, and he received it in good part; a second time did likewise, but said, 'you have talked enough to me about religion, don't speak to me about it any more—I won't bear it, and shall knock you down.' I passed his shops to-day, and the chance was so good I urged him to seek the Lord at once, to make sure work for heaven without delay. He flew into a passion and turned a whole battery of curses upon me. It seemed he would bounce me whether or no. But I finished my message to him and left it with the Lord."

This incident happened but a few hours after the other. The other may have inspired it, for men strengthen one another in an evil way, little dreaming that not their bravadoes give them impunity in encroaching upon the pure, but that to them unthinkable something called grace. In a few days the haughty man sickened, and in a few more I heard one say to another, "Mr. Blank died this morning about four o'clock." I said to him privately as the train leaped along its journey, "did he say anything of Mr. Willis before he died?" "Yes," he replied, "with others I waited on him, doing all that friends could to prevent death. He said he was very sorry he had been rude to Mr. Willis and hoped God would forgive him for it, that Mr. Willis was one of the best men in the world and was trying to do him good when he railed at him so—he was much distressed about it."

But to our story.

Miller Willis' respect for woman was nice. To him she dwelt in the realm of reverence. When he spoke to her there were fluty notes in his naturally grating voice, like the music of a song when the singer smothers every note save the clearest, yet tenderest. He seldom forgot the conventionals that hedge her in. But passing a street in S——, he beheld a lady looking from a window at some flowers, and, eager for souls, he said, "have you been converted, and do you know it? No conversion, no place in the kingdom of heaven. You must be converted!"

She drew back from observation; but Miller had made no pause as he loosed the divine message to fly with its warning, like the carrier-dove, to her window. She quivered with indignation that one had dared address her from the stacet, and when her husband got home from the store, she told him the incident, describing the man.

"That's all right, love," he said, "the man is Miller Willis from Augusta; he's going with Brother Bigham round the district. He's the last one that would offend you. It's his way to help souls to God."

"It's a rude way," she replied. "We are both members of the church, and attentive to religious duties. Why should the man have asked that question of me more than of another?"

"Well, love," he answered, "if you had been on the streets to-day you rather would have wondered to whom he didn't address that question. He lets none pass unwarned; he keeps busy about the Master's business, you may be sure. No use to be displeased about it—he meant the best. Since you have been telling me about it, I've been asking myself the question, 'Am I really converted? Have we ever been converted?'"

So they conversed, turning the question o'er and o'er in their minds, and agreeing it was worth praying about with and for each other, they began together to seek to know for themselves the hidden power of God's love. In preaching Sunday, my heart was strangely moved to invite penitents to the altar; "but it is communion day," I objected, "Bishop Pierce and his father are present; they will think it untimely—the service will be too long, people become impatient." The impression became imperative, so I gave the call for penitents, and Bro. —— and his good wife were the first to come weeping to the mercy seat. There was a quiver in the congregation, for few, if any, were more consistent members than they.

A few services afterward I saw them both converted. They had come forward for prayer every invitation. Service was about to close that night when Sister —— rose up, clasped her hands, her face shining with rapture, a strange charm in every movement, and said softly, "I'm converted! I'm so happy. Praise God! I know I'm converted." She went to a lady or two and embraced them, and turned eagerly looking across the church; her husband rose to his feet, she flitted round the altar towards him, he opened his arms, they were together—both happy—both converted in almost the same moment. And what of Miller Willis?

Miller sat on the front amen bench. Face turned a little towards heaven glowing with joy, all unconscious of the part he had wrought in their conversion, saying, "Amen! Praise God. That's the kind, I know I'm converted! No hope so about that!" But next morning in experience meeting they told of Miller and his question. How it led them to see their true state—unconverted, and how its impressions had moved them to constant prayer for converting grace till it had come to them, and now they were happy on the way, and thanked God they ever heard Miller ask the question, "have you ever been converted?"

It was shortly after the incidents narrated, I was standing on the court-house steps in W——, and saw several groups of men part and hurriedly disappear from the square. An irreligious merchant beckoned me across to him and said: "Did you see those men shying off like deer into the stores? They took fright at Miller as he appeared on the street. I have been telling about cases at ——; they were afraid he would talk to them and they'd forget and cuss him, and God would kill them; that's why they got away so quick."

The next day he said, "Come in here, I've something to tell you. I was at my desk just now writing; a big, clever drummer was leaning just here against the counter. I heard Miller say, 'Have you ever been converted?' I expected a scene and dropped my pen to be ready. Miller was in the street near the door. The drummer said nothing, but eyed him up and down. Miller waited till he got his look out, and said, 'The soul that sinneth it shall die. You must be born of the spirit. Have you ever been converted?' The drummer looked him over and over and over, and said: 'No, I've never been converted, and when I am it will not be by one of your damned sort either.' 'Never mind that,' said Miller, lifting his hand towards the sky, 'that's nothing to do with it. Verily, I say unto you, except ye be converted and become as little children, ye cannot enter the kingdom of God. You must be converted!' and walked on. I stepped to the drummer and said, "You ought not to have spoken to that man as you did, he's every body's friend. Do you know him?"

"No," he replied, "and don't want to."

"Well," said I, "I know him—went to school with him; and several years ago, if you had looked at him and spoken to him as you did, you would have been the worse thrashed man in half a minute that's been in this place since the war."

"Ah! that's a game two can play at," he replied. "That little fellow whip me?"

"Yes," said I, "pawed up the earth with you till you thought a cyclone had you. He's a religious man now. Besides, some men cursed him the other day, and they are dead and buried. God resents things for him now. You had best hunt him up and ask his pardon before you leave for the way you treated him."

"S——," he said, "you know me; true I sell goods for a wholesale liquor house, but I respect religion, and religious persons. I never saw this strange man before; if I had known who he was I would not have spoken to him as I did."

The man was really alarmed, and tried to find Miller to ask his pardon.

CHAPTER XV.

Miller had little taste for any thing except the spiritual—religious. He looked in at the door upon an annual conference once in Augusta. The usual hum of voices, papers and motion were going on; a minute satisfied him, and exclaiming "Eh" in capitals and double emphasis, which put the preachers near the door in an uproar of laughter, he was gone.

He avoided, on the round, quarterly conference sessions—too much business—religious. He'd get out in a grove or sequestered nook to read and pray till they were adjourned. But he came in when we were nearly through once, and took a seat among those brethren on the right of the altar. We were puzzling over the minimum paid to the preacher, and the heavy balance yet due by the several churches on the circuit. I noticed presently a flutter next to Miller. Three brethren had their heads down behind the benches quivering; one flattened himself into the corner, yet swelled and puffed and held his cheeks; one sat rigid as marble, hand tightly clasped over his mouth, eyes dancing with mirth; another looking fiercely into Miller's face. I knew at a glance they had a case; a side issue that threatened all—except Miller and the angry one—with convulsions. I said something "foreign to the subject" to help them to self-restraint, and they did very well a while. But soon a mighty whispering went on there that made me know that corner was flushed anew; then Miller spoke in low, distinct tones: "My! starving your preacher—keeping back his own from him; making him work for you in the gospel and support himself. It's a shame to gamblers even. Your church paid less than fifty dollars all the year! Why, the poor factory people in Augusta do a heap better than that. You ought to pay that much yourself, and then be doing no great thing. You are all backslid, if you ever had any religion. Go right up there and pay your church out like a man!" There was a jumpy thud—the big, tall man had leaped to his feet and was gazing down into Miller's quiet, firm face with a look of utter disgust and wrath, then pressed his way out the door, saying: "I won't stay in here—I'll hear no such. The others pulled their noses, clutched their hair, clasped their mouths, looked at Miller, and in the effort not to laugh out in meeting, their benches shook like an earthquake had them. Without knowing it he had attacked the miser of the crowd, and told him things that had never before entered into his philosophy—things his brethren had longed for him to hear but dared not utter. Amid the very merriment he provoked, Miller had won their hearts and they rallied to the question.

He was an original—none like him in all the earth. Men laughed and shouted for joy because of him in the same breath. His abruptness, unconscious courage, directness, peculiarities of manner and emphasis, giving the devil his due while stirring souls to God in season, out of season, one way and another and forever, imparted a fresh, new, quick, varied spell upon the best and the worst. Had he not been just himself—only Miller Willis—he would have been but a derisive eccentric; but as he was himself alone full of God, wherever he appeared men soon knew there was a strange king in the camp—however peculiar, none the less a very king of men. That his abruptness was sometimes met with abruptions, is no marvel when men's nature is remembered. I said to him once: "Miller, have you never been smitten in approaching men?"

"Yes," he replied, "five times knocked nearly down; but what is that to saving a soul? Once in speaking to a crowd of gamblers of their sin, one of them struck me quick as a mule kicks. I didn't know but some of the rest would tear him in pieces before they would heed me and let him alone."

In elegant Eatonton, I missed him awhile after dinner, and thinking my presence would favor his work on the streets, I went there. I saw as I neared the square the excitement was up. A group of lawyers was discussing him, while looking down a principal thoroughfare, the store doors were full of gazers. Many had stepped into the street, strung out across it like the muster-line of Judge Longstreet's "Georgia Scenes," peering in the same direction—it was their first sight of Miller. I heard afar off the call, "have you ever been converted? Ye must be converted. Turn ye, turn ye, for why will ye die. I wonder if there's any backsliders here? Be sure your sins will find you out," and I knew Miller was there and safe. In greeting me one of the lawyer group said: "Mr. Bigham, who the—the—is that man?"

It was easy enough to read the word hell between lines of this question, but the questioner had flushed good-humoredly at coming so near and just missing it, and I queried, "Whom do you mean?" "Why," he replied, "that little black-headed dump of a preacher that's got the whole town stirred up, agog, watching him like he were the lunatic asylum turned loose, and flying at his approach like the devil were after them?"

"It's Miller Willis," I replied; "not a preacher, a layman come to help us in a meeting. Goodness will not exactly die when he does, but a heap of it will leave the world at that time."

Just then the men in the street and store doors fled to cover; one of my group slid into the office, two stood their ground till Miller came up and were introduced to him, and stood fairly to his exhortations until he turned from us into another street. No man assailed him with hot words intolerant, polite Eatonton. They laughed at themselves and one another among themselves concerning him. But many, unused to religious thoughts, took his works of fire into their bosoms to think over, and many Christians were quickened by his presence.

I said to the members of the quarterly conference, at its close, "Miller Willis' expenses are something on this journey among the churches. You are under no obligation whatever about them, but if your hearts are free to it, and you wish it, I will hand him any present you will bestow. True, it will do him, personally, little good. He will give it away to the poor, but it is a huge joy for him to give, and he deserves it."

"Yes," replied one of the finest characters that ever graced the church or State, "we'll do cheerfully anything you say, but I fear it was a mistake to bring him for the meeting's good—not adapted to our people." Several hands dashed for their pockets as he spoke, and one said, "give him that bill for me, Brother B., he's done me that much good anyhow," "and that," said another, "he's done me five times its good," "and that and that," said others. A soft smile scuffled through the pastor's face (W. D. Anderson) at the rapid scene of tears and liberality, as he added his offering.

"Well," said the doubter, as he cheerily added his gift, "I am the mistaken one; you have made no mistake at all in bringing him. I take the criticism all back; our preachers always know best about these things. Miller has done good it seems to every man in this room, the very leaders in the church." "Yes, interjected one, "you've not been well enough to be about the streets much of late, and you'd be surprised to hear the many persons in and out of any church, say how much good he has done them—the best and the hardest speak of it."

He had made the mistake men of his rank were apt to make at first concerning Miller and his methods, forgetful for the time, that in elegance there are avenues admitting and admiring just the character, when fully discerned, now before him, needing its presence to make even itself wiser, nobler, happier, better. This does not apply to the imaginary elegant; they are "mistaken souls"—weak; nor to the exquisites, they are dudes.

Of the sensibilities, Miller possessed a rare one—perhaps the grace of delicacy best defines it. Many, not knowing if there be any grace of delicacy, a sweetest pearl in his wondrous make-up, hindered the matchless worker by thrusting themselves forward when an angel would stand aside lest he obstruct him who lives on heaven's verge constantly.

I do not recall the date, my district book being misplaced, of the Richmond camp-meeting when he entered the sanctified state; but it was about fifteen years ago, and in the scope of vines and woods to the right of the camp-ground as it is entered from Augusta. Though he said he did, I doubt that he ever lost the grace; only lost the witnessing glory, and he always specially loved Rev. W. C. Dunlap who guided him again into the reassured experience. Thenceforward he professed it unmistakably, irrepressibly, jubilantly. Like lightning clapping its hands in cloudy and clear weather were his avowels of holiness. He was a strict Biblicist, and loved to call it *sanctification* in emphasized capitals, yet professed it as distinctively "the second blessing." He often was expecting certain persons to obtain it, and said of a few: "They have it if they'd just say so." He lived it. No vision of a season, no brainsick theory was it with him. It was as real as Mt. Pisgah, and, like its sacred height, brought him close to heaven. His was a softer, more lovingly sympathetic character after this experience came to him. Before it, he was the Jewish prophet (he looked like a Jew) exclaiming, "Thou art the man! repent or be turned into hell." Now he was more the good Samaritan binding up his wounds who "fell among thieves," and was left "stripped, wounded, half dead."

Last summer he came to us at the Dalton parsonage from some meetings near, and for a week helped us in the great tabernacle meeting. Every where at first appearance, a certain dread of him fell upon the people—a wonderment such as I imagine souls feel when nearest the supernatural; they preferred a space between him and them. Young people of either sex, even of religious habit and experience, were apt to yield to the weird emotion till better acquainted, when wonder of him joined with reverencing joy for his presence, and the fascination of his exclamations and appeals.

Dalton is equaled by few cities in young ladies whose education and Christian culture excel. One of these, in passing the parsonage, paused, as was her wont, to greet its inmates, and was invited to come in. "O, no, no!" she said, with eyes amazed, yet smiling, "I cannot call until your company leaves." "We have no company," was replied, "except Brother Willis, and he's up-stairs in his room likely praying for you now." "Well," she said, "I mean specially him. I don't want to meet him

—I'm afraid of him, he's like some strange being, not mortal. I might say something not exactly right, but as he's shut in up-stairs I'll come in awhile."

Just as she stepped upon the veranda Miller appeared at the door, and throwing up her hands, she exclaimed, "O, there he is now! I must g—go; good-bye," and sped away. Miller, with his quaint emphasis, said: "Eh! what is that for!" "She's afraid to meet you," was answered; and Miller exclaimed after her, "the wicked flee when no man pursueth!" But she made no tarrying in all the plain—her charming face flushing more and more with the confusion of hearing and flight.

"Mr. Willis," said my wife, "that's one of the most lovable Christians in all the world—few excel her in any way. She'd be a martyr for her church and pastors, and twice such for the Christ." "Well," replied Miller, "the text will do her good anyhow, it's the Lord's word." And it was for good. For in speaking of it afterwards, she said: "While it frightened me more, it was so unexpected and apt, that it made me laugh and cry almost in the same instant. Now I am more afraid to fly from than to meet him, and I intend being a better Christian, less like the wicked." She set herself a hard task in the last two phrases, for Prov. xxxi:29, applies apter to her than to one among a thousand. And surely never was man more perfectly furnished with the "apt words fitly spoken" of God's book than he. The "apples of gold" were tossed into the heart by him forevermore, except when "polished arrows" were used by him.

In going from the house into the city he usually paused as he closed the gate, and lifted his right hand towards heaven seemingly in deep thought. My wife said to him once in that attitude, "Mr. Willis, why do you, in starting up town always pause at the gate and lift your hand up toward heaven?"

"O," he answered, "I am just asking the good Lord to tell me which way to go to meet the right persons and do the most good." And just then, glancing across the beautiful avenue, he beheld two young ladies watering flowers from the hydrant over there. He whirled instantly away, crossed the street to them, and before they knew he was near, said: "Have you ever been converted? You must be born of the spirit—except ye be converted and become as little children, ye shall not enter into the kingdom of heaven!"

One of them fled into the house; the other wanted to, but couldn't get disentangled from the flowers and the watering hose, and replied: "I don't know, sir, if I have been converted. I am a member of the Presbyterian church."

"That won't do," he said; "people may be church members and not ready for Heaven. You must be converted, born from above."

She stood like some fair vision, trembling in the interview as he urged her to seek till she knew she was converted, and turned away towards the church. She said after he had gone she kept thinking of the words, "have you ever been converted. You must be converted till you know it;" in the house and out among the flowers, everywhere, the very tones in which they were uttered singing constantly in her heart till she went to the tabernacle altar, and sought that special grace. It came to her rich, enrapturing, full. She came to me amid the weeping and song, and hosanna of the altar, to tell me of it, saying, in wondering ecstasy, "O, I'm converted. I'm converted. It came to me while praying, so joyously and sweet! It is so happy to be converted—to know I am the Lord's." She looked, in her laughing tears of gratitude, to God for His saving grace, like an impersoned dream in whose visions faith, peace, heavenly hope, unspeakable joy and love, had woven their gladdest colors of bliss. Her name was Lily, and divine grace had now arrayed her in a beauty more charming than the power of her name, "the beauty of holiness."

How many like instances of Miller's strange wooing to Christ lie asleep in Jesus, wherever he went, waiting the resurrection of the just, or yet live adorning the doctrine of holiness to the Lord!

In speaking of incidents that befell him in the country churches around Dalton, he said: "I noticed a lady in the congregation who all the while seemed indifferent to the services, so I thought I'd urge her to seek religion and be saved. In talking to her about it, I asked her if she had ever been converted. She said it was none of my business, and wished I would let her alone, which closed the conversation, of course. But another time the impression to persuade her to turn to God and live was so strong that I did so the best I knew how. With angry exclamations, quick as thought, she slapped my face r-rap! So I said: 'I shall leave you in the care of the Lord,' and left her."

"Shame, shame!" exclaimed the ladies in the parlor. "And does she live after that?"

"I hope so," said Miller, smiling, "but she made my ears ring and my cheek tingle. I reckon one might have seen the print of her full hand on my cheek for minutes after. I believe she was deeply convicted for sin, why she became so furious; maybe she'll be converted soon."

"Miller forever," thought I, "gallant as a knight to the last; he hoped all things good of woman, even against hope, and he's right."

This brings the query, "why did so many he talked to about their souls, particularly as he stressed the appeal 'you *must* be converted, and *now* is the time,' go beside themselves with rage, and here and there with cursing?" Is the answer in this—their *unspirituality* was bitter, perfect; his spirituality intense, perfect, "the single mind," and so the battle to the death was at once on—"Michael contending with the devil about the body of Moses." But like the angel, it was not Miller that railed and winced, whatever the devil did.

After no conflict of the sort did I ever hear him say, "The Lord rebuke him," but "The Lord save him." Once he said to me, "while the cursing man was ripping around so, I felt, "old fellow, if j-u-s-t the Lord was willing, I'd soon make you sing another song to that," but the feeling was only for a moment, and I *was ashamed of myself* that it found a moment's space in me." What power is in the grace that made Miller Willis, naturally fierce and quick as a cyclone, forbearing and patient as love! Should we not all have grace of that special power—ministers and laymen—it martyrs self to spare and bless others?

It was current, even before he professed sanctification, that more than a dozen men who had viciously cursed him, as he besought them to turn from evil to good, had quickly gone down in strange deaths as though smitten by the invisible God. "Shall not Shimei be put to death for this, because he cursed the Lord's anointed?" Miller, like David, spared Shimei, but God rested not till the fearful doom overtook him.

Miller had with him at Dalton, in that lumbersome black satchel, a record book. One day he said to my little daughter, Lewie, "you must write for me to-day in my book. I am storing away in it some things in my life which, maybe, the Lord will bless to souls after I am in Heaven, if I ever get there, less than the least, less than the least, yet I am in the way, bless the Lord." But when the set time to write as he should utter came, he said: "I cannot attend to the book to-day; I must go about and try to save some souls."

I wish the entries in that book could be read, especially by those who knew him best. Doubtless they are simple and pure as light, flooded with heavenly life.

Once, just before he went on the streets to seek souls, we grouped about him as he stood clasping his long staff like one which that national celebrity, General Duff Green, used in his latter days, my wife queried: "Do you still fast and pray every Sunday for Major Willis as you did when you came to see us in Middle Georgia?"

"No," he replied, with a smile of utter joy, "Brother Ed. is converted now. He was always a big-hearted, good brother. I shall meet him in Heaven; for if I ever get there, I shall see Brother Ed. there. If he goes first he'll greet me among the first when I come; if I go first I know I'll be on the edge to welcome him. There's no put on about Brother Ed.; he meant to live right. But I am fasting and praying now for another person every Sunday. I hope the Lord will save that person, too; if not while I live, some time sure, anyhow." And he passed out to the sidewalk, going to seek and persuade the lost to Christ.

At the tabernacle, the night before he left for Atlanta and Oconee county to help in meetings, I had a few words with two old Confederate veterans who knew him in the war, and at the depot next morning they handed me a new purse for him with about twenty dollars in it, which grew to about thirty as he stepped upon the cars. Presently he was casting pearls among the throngs about the train, and as the engine pulled along in careful start away, he rounded up his exhortation as follows: "I wonder who's got religion! Without holiness no man shall see the Lord! You must be converted and *sancti-*

fied, too, and know it—not hope so. You can have a hope and yet be lost. Where is the backslider! Let him return unto the Lord and He will have mercy upon him. 'The wicked shall be turned into hell, and all the nations that forget God.'"

So he exclaimed as the cars rolled away, and I watched him out of sight, not thinking it was my last look at Miller Willis, strange as an incarnate phantom, as perfect a Christian spirit as ever I knew on land or sea. No marvel that Mr. Adams, in his touching narrative of his death scene in Spantanburg, S. C., says: "He was cold, and his eyes almost set; he could not see me, but he could hear my voice and understand me. I said: 'Are you still trusting in the Lord?' 'Now and forever,' he replied, and then asked, 'do you hear me?' 'Yes, praise the Lord!' I said, and with 'amen' on his lips, he died. It seemed to me that when he asked if I heard him, his spirit had already crossed over the river, and, standing on the shore of paradise, he called back to know if I could hear his last testimony for Christ."

CHAPTER XVI.

IMPRESSIONS OF MILLER WILLIS, BY REV. C. C. CARY, OF THE NORTH GA. CONFERENCE, M. E. CHURCH, SOUTH.

No layman in religious circles was better known in Georgia and South Carolina than Miller Willis. No one was more greatly beloved, and no life left a finer influence and made a deeper impression for good. "He being dead, yet speaketh." No death was more deeply regretted—not that we would change the order of Providence, but because it seems as if such a man could hardly be spared.

For Miller Willis I had a peculiar affection. My relation to him was one of intimacy for many years. I knew much of his inner life. At the Houghton Institute in Augusta, Ga., we were school-boys together, though he was several years my senior. When in September, 1867, I joined St. James' Church, Augusta, I was thrown immediately in close contact with him, and he became my companion and adviser. No one did more to influence my life and shape my Christian character. Whatever is aggressive in my religious composition is due largely to early and intimate association with this godly man. He taught me lessons not learned in books. Together, as young men, we visited the jail and city hospital to talk to and pray with the inmates. Together we went into the houses of the poor and rooms of the sick, and sat up with the dead. Weekly in class-meetings and young men's prayer-meeting, we were thrown in contact with each other. He was one of the few who heard my first prayer in public, and was present when I first led a public service. Often did we hold sweet converse together in those days. Of late years I did not see as much of him, but our relations were still intimate.

His conversion was of the "sky-blue" kind. Nothing could make him doubt it. How often have I heard him, in public and in private, speak of the time so distinct and the place so marked on Ellis street, Augusta, Ga., just across from his home, where God, for Christ's sake, converted his soul! How he immediately went around and woke up the neighbors to tell them the glad news, and how slow they were to believe that he who had been so wild and mischievous, should be saved from sin! That fact he never doubted. That moment never faded from his memory.

Then, several years thereafter, he was entirely sanctified at Richmond county camp-meeting, but soon lost the experience. Afterward at White Oak church in Columbia county, under a sermon by Rev. W. C. Dunlap, he again received this grace of sanctification, which he retained till he died. No man gave clearer testimony to the two great facts in religious experience of spiritual regeneration and entire sanctification.

It is not often a man is announced as dead and lives

to read his own obituary, but such was the case with him fifteen years ago. On February 27, 1876, the *Augusta Constitutionalist* published his death as having occurred in Charleston, S. C., the day before, and announced that his body would arrive that afternoon for burial. Much to the joy of many friends, the news was contradicted two days later. God had further use for him, and, as in the case of old Hezekiah, added fifteen years to his life.

Our departed brother was remarkable in several particulars. Like King Saul, he was head and shoulders above many of the people about him, in faith, in zeal and in consecration. In these respects, however, there is no reason why many might not be like him. His strong faith, constant devotion and burning zeal may be duplicated. Divine sovereignty does not forbid it.

Several things deeply impress me concerning Brother Willis:

Men regarded him as "peculiar," and in some respects he was. But it was not because he coveted peculiarity. He had no foolish ambition to be regarded as queer. Whatever of peculiarity there was about him, was the natural result of his deep religious convictions, his abiding faith in and fixed purpose to conform his life to God's Word. He was so far ahead of those about him in entire devotion to God, that it made him seem peculiar. If more of us were more Christ-like, as he was, his seeming peculiarity would not have been so striking, while the world might have also called us peculiar. He was unlike the world around him, and just so far was he really peculiar. Miller Willis never did anything solely that he might be singular. There was "method in his madness." If he ever did anything out of the usual order, there was some noble end in view. If on the street, in the family or in the church, he did anything which seemed strange or out of the usual order of things, it was that he might impress or save a soul or please God. If he had a mania for any one thing, it was to pull souls out of the fire. And much of his so-called peculiarities grew out of this burning desire to save men. If he knelt in prayer before eating, or on entering a church, it was that he believed literally in praying everywhere and over everything, and that he should not be ashamed to kneel before men. If he questioned persons on the highway about their souls, or in the home circle, it was because he believed religion should be an every-day subject of conversation, and no time was ill-timed to talk to dying men and women about their eternal interests. Misunderstood? Of course he was. But so was his Lord. Not appreciated? Neither was his great forerunner, the Apostle Paul. Doing things out of the regular order? Yes; and so did his predecessor, John Wesley.

No greater mistake was made than when some people thought him crazy. On any subject he would converse intelligently at proper times. It was only necessary to have him in the home circle to know him as he really was—clear-headed and sensible, tender-hearted and true. He had no time to waste on the world's trivial affairs.

When on his Master's business, he was too sharp to be switched off of his favorite theme of salvation by the sinner whom he was warning to flee from the wrath to come. How did he know but that this would be the last warning this dying soul would ever receive?

Men called him "cranky." But in the revelations of the judgment it need not surprise us if Miller Willis shows up as the wisest of all those who thus spoke of him on the earth.

He was noted for his strong faith in prayer. Who can tell how much he prayed? If God gave him access to human hearts—if he had power with men—if he had a religious influence which had weight—it was because he went often to the closet and tarried long at the mercy seat. He knew the source of power. He knew how to pray. Here was one great secret of his life—a secret easily discovered to all, but apparently hidden from many. The "hour of prayer" was a familiar one. It was an hour of wrestling, of communion, of delight. He discovered what so many forget, that the true source of strength was not in worldly wisdom or wealth—not in human knowledge or social prestige, but in God; and nothing could prove a substitute for prayer.

He was remarkable for his simple and implicit faith in a special Providence. No little child ever trusted his earthly parent more than Miller Willis confided in his Heavenly Father. And no little child was ever more tenderly cared for by father and mother than was Miller Willis by his Father in heaven. If all his life were known, there would appear as remarkable things as ever occurred in the history of George Muller. Some things were so surprising that no explanation is satisfactory save on the ground of a special Providence. Miller Willis' life was a standing proof and clear illustration of this Scripture doctrine.

His was a special mission to warn sinners and call them to repentance. Possibly no man in Georgia, whether minister or layman, ever warned more souls of the wrath to come, in public and in private, in religious meetings, in the homes of the people, and on the highway. Wherever he went, in city or country, there his voice was heard, in warning tones, calling out to men to turn from sin and be saved. This one thing he never forgot. The "care of souls" was ever on his heart. He always remembered that wherever he met his fellowmen some one might receive his last warning at his mouth. If the story of his frequent warnings could be written, with the sequel in each case, how our hearts would be moved!

What was the secret of his life? He believed implicitly God's Word and lived as if he believed it. And others believed that he believed it. Only this and nothing more. He held fast to the doctrine of eternal punishment. He never became so worldly-wise and advanced in theology as to modify the Scripture teaching about an everlasting hell. He believed sinners were on the verge of eternal torment, and went up and down the earth warning men of their imminent peril.

He was no sponge. He was always giving out something good. To be with him was to be blessed. He absorbed much of God's grace, but only God knows how much he gave out. He had no regular income, yet never lacked for any good thing. Still he never asked man for a cent. Of all he received, he gave back one-half to the Lord. A favorite expression with him was, "Behold, Lord, the half of my goods I give to the poor." Though seemingly dependent, he was not. There was something manly and noble about him, and numbers were only too glad to favor him.

Thank God for Miller Willis! Heaven is richer and earth is poorer. "His works do follow him." The good world seems much nearer since he has gone to live there. He is not a stranger to its inhabitants. While my heart is strangely sad at the thought that he is gone from us, and we shall see his face no more on earth, it is cheered with the blessed hope that he is forever with the Lord.

How he longed to "depart and be with Christ!" Those who knew him best know how anxious for years he was to go. Never soured, neither repining nor fretting about earth; always happy, cheerful and submissive, whatever his lot might be; he realized truly he was only a stranger and pilgrim, and was " willing rather to be absent from the body and be present with the Lord." How he roams over heaven's fair fields and revels in its holy joys and angelic associations! None more joyous than he—none sing louder notes of praise to his Redeeming Lord! At last he has gained that place of which he so often sang and about which he delighted to talk!

Will he not watch and wait at Heaven's gate for those of us he has left behind? The thought of Miller Willis in heaven almost makes me long to go over the river and be with him.

A member of the Georgia Legislature, a companion and schoolmate of Miller Willis in his boyhood days, and a member of the same church, said to me a few days after his death, that if what we believe in the Scriptures is true, there could be no doubt that when Miller Willis' redeemed and disembodied spirit left this earth for the better world, the everlasting gates swung wide open to allow him an abundant entrance, and the angels and the spirits of just men made perfect accorded him a grand and hearty welcome. And who that knew him doubts it?

Augusta honored herself in giving him such a funeral. Its cemetery holds no dust more precious and sacred. "Thy brother shall live again!"

It is no mere poetic sentiment, but truth we may sing over his grave:

> "Servant of God, well done!
> Rest from thy loved employ;
> The battle fought, the victory won;
> Enter thy Master's joy."

CLEMENT C. CARY.

Atlanta, Ga., Sept. 12, 1891.

CHAPTER XVII.

MILLER WILLIS.

[From Rev. M. D. Smith, of the North Georgia Conference.]

I had known this precious man for five or six years. I am not quite sure, but think I first met him at Griffin in a Holiness Convention (where he always was when it was within reach of him).

While everybody I ever heard speak of him said he was crazy, I was wonderfully drawn to him, and was delighted with his dead shots on sin. He impressed me as no other man ever did. I never tired of his company. I have had him in my home weeks at a time and he was always a welcome guest. In 1890 he spent some months in Atlanta, and most of his time was divided between the home of Bro. Thos. Thrower and myself. It was during this stay that he had his famous bible rebound, and the first entry, or note he made in it, after the blank leaves were put in, was in my study. I can see him as he would sit near me by a window, pen and ink in readiness, with some book busy reading, suddenly he would exclaim, "Bless God I have an idea!" and then with haste he would transfer it to his Bible under some appropriate text. I would sometimes say, "Bro. Willis, what is your new idea?" "Ah, I can't give you my thunder, you would use it the first chance you had," he said. "I was down with Bro. Reese some time ago, and he would get hold of my Bible and get some of my best thoughts, and just when I would think of bringing them forth, bless the goodness, Bro. Reese would turn loose the very thing I had in mind to say, and I would wonder where he got that. I knew I had never read or heard any man use that thought but myself, and I come to find out he had been stealing my thunder, and I just put my Bible beyond his reach, and that is the way I will have to do you." One of his pat sayings, when he would begin his study was, "Now I am going into meditations most profound, and the first fellow who disturbs me will just come down with a V-dollar bill." Accompanying the remark with a slap on my knee, and many would be the V (ve) dollar bills he would have to pay, had we kept count against him, for before five minutes he would have some idea to air.

One remarkable fact was, the children all liked him. I would know sometimes before he was near the house by the little ones crying, "Oh, yonder comes Brother Willis!" and then away to see who could get to him first. He always would inquire if they loved Jesus. I remember one day he had the whole crop out in the hall teaching them to repeat in concert 1st John 2d chapter and 1st verse, "My little children, these things write I unto you, that ye sin not," and never did he stop until the last little toddler who could talk could repeat the whole text and tell where it was found.

He had a peculiarity of giving the chapter and verse

in all his quotations. I never saw Brother Willis in too big a hurry to stop to speak to some man about his soul, and to give him a tract. When he and I had to go anywhere together I always started in time to allow him time to talk some by the way. He, wife and I were going to Trinity one night to church, and I am sure he did not pass a single bar-room that he did not walk into it with the air of a king, and right up to the counter and square himself before the bar-tender and give him a tract. Many times it would be his favorite exhortation, which he had printed in large red letters— "PREPARE TO MEET THY GOD." The fellow would be most sure to ask, "What is this?" His ready answer was, "A message from God for you, sir," and often without another word he would walk out, and every time he put his right foot on the floor the pilgrim staff would strike it at the same instant.

He and I went often together to a tent meeting held on Mangum street, under direction of Brother W. P. Smith. One German had a little beer shop on the back street, and Brother Willis never passed the man without stopping. The first time he went in the old fellow said, very pleasantly, in his dialect, "What will you have?" When Miller handed him his "PREPARE TO MEET THY GOD" and said, "You are dealing out damnation here to your fellow man," etc., when the little German said, "Gits ride oud o' my leedle shoup, I tells you! I vants no sich coostomer." But Brother Willis had thrown his arrow and was quite ready to go. The next night it was quite in order for him to enter again, and he popped his head in at the door and said, "Your door has this sign, 'OPEN, COME IN,' and I am in," and down went another tract on the counter and the irate Dutchman vociferating, "Gits ride out o' my leedle shoup!" The third night he gave him another call, the dutchy decided he would change his manner, so, when Brother Willis entered he said, "Walk ride oup and have a leedle something to drink." Brother Willis said, "Bless God, I have a fountain within me springing up unto eternal life —won't you drink of it and stop gulping down this vile stuff you have here?" "Gits ride out o' my leedle shoup—gits ride out I tell you, I have de police after you, you insults a man ride in his own house." "Yes, but he that being often reproved and hardeneth his neck shall suddenly be destroyed, and that without remedy." That was the last time he ever entered that beer shop— the fire in a day or two thereafter fixed it in bad shape for any one to enter.

One day, about this time, he came in hurriedly and said, "Bro. Smith, I have come to get some tracts printed to suit the dear bar-keepers." I have forgotten the form, but it was mainly scriptures, such as this: "Woe unto him who puts the bottle to his neighbors' lips," etc. He made it quite personal and practical. You may depend I printed him the required number, and away he went, and never stopped till he had put one in every bar-room he could find in Atlanta. He then came back for another, saying, "I have put in the probe, now I want to pour in oil and wine and see if I can get them to the inn." This one he had more mild, yet very pointed. When supplied, away he went on his second round to visit the "dear bar-keepers," as he termed them. A few days afterward a bar-keeper on Marietta street fell dead in his place of business, and a citizen told me that that man had abused and cursed Miller Willis a few days before, when he was in to see him.

He gave away more tracts than any man I ever knew, and never threw one away, but would pick up one if he saw some one else throw it away.

One night the matress factory on corner of Marietta and Foundry streets burned; it made a tremendous fire, and this was a hey-day with Bro. Willis; he told me he sowed tracts around that fire by the hundreds, and exhorted them to "flee the fire of hell, which was a thousand times worse than this on which they were looking."

I am indebted to him for all the good I may ever do by printing and distributing tracts; it was through him, as an instrument, that I first saw the good possible to be accomplished by scattering tracts. "Bread upon the waters to be gathered after many days." Not being able to buy as many as I wanted, I bought an outfit to print for myself and give to others at a low price. May God ever bless the life-work of the dear man.

I knew that he was on the decline, but did not expect the end to come so soon. He went with me to assist Brother E. M. Stanton on the Dalton Circuit, 1890, and while there I first realized how weak he was. He would walk two hundred yards from his boarding house to the arbor where we held meetings, and would take hold in the altar service with all his might and work as of yore, but before the service was over often he would have to retire, and maybe not be able to attend again that day. I had hoped that rest would restore in a measure at least his strength. He was one man who was literally worn out in the Lord's work. He told me since he had started out to work for the Lord he had not made a dollar, with one exception. While on a stay in Charleston, some religious paper or magazine wanted him to collect for them, and he did enough at that to make a few dollars, and only did that to have a chance to get into homes and talk to them of salvation. He told me while with me that when he started from Augusta some brother there gave him $15 and another $25, and later in the day another gave him some amount, I forget just what, but he for once put $25 in the bank. [I made the deposit myself for him.—ED.] "I am not sure," said he, "but I have done wrong, for God gave it to me for His work, and I laid it up. He does not want me to lay up anything, and I think I shall send and get it and put it out to interest, so He will not accuse me of burying my Lord's money." I guess he did so. He was not a spendthrift, but was careful and quite economical. While with me I noticed often when he was in the act of kneeling down he would twist his pants legs a little to one side or the other at the knee. Said I, "Brother Willis, why do you thus twist your pants?" "Oh," said he, "I always wear a hole first in the knee, and I am trying to avoid it in these!"

I never saw him eat a meal without first kneeling and asking God's blessing, and often when called on to ask a blessing would repeat some verse of Scripture, and if not called on would say something anyway. At the conclusion of the meal, dinner for instance, he would say, "Thank God, we have eaten our dinner and are still alive, bless His holy name."

I asked him why he took up this habit. Said he, "I have been more or less associated with the Salvation Army, and I saw they did so, and was impressed with the idea, and it grew on me. The devil flouted me with it and said, 'You would be odd and people would remark about it, and then you could as well say what you had to say sitting and silent.' I had to get the victory over satan, and could not allow a Salvation soldier to be more humble than I, for I loved Jesus as well as he, and was as thankful as he, and would do as much to express it. Furthermore, it caused the Salvation soldiers to be persecuted." While he was not courting persecution, he knew there was something in it if it made the devil mad. Said he thought often it gave a more serious direction to the conversation during the meal than otherwise would have been, and he felt he was honoring God by so doing, for the grace is too often said more for form than for anything else.

He was rigid in his observance of the Sabbath day, and often he would take a two mile walk in his feeble health to get to church rather than ride on the street cars. He would yell at the top of his voice at the driver as he would pass to "Remember the Sabbath day to keep it holy." If he could get close to a car on a switch he would give the passengers an exhortation, telling them they were forcing men to stay away from God's house to accommodate them; that the drivers wanted to go to church as bad as they, but had to drive for their accommodation.

CHAPTER XVIII.

Letter from Rev. T. B. Reynolds, of the Florida Conference, M. E. Church, South.

Welborn, Fla., Aug. 6, 1891.

Rev. W. C. Dunlap, Augusta, Ga.:

Dear Bro.—I have just been reading this morning in the *Way of Life*, of the death and burial, etc., of that precious man of God, Miller Willis. I would read awhile and cry awhile. I considered him one of the best men I ever met. I am like Bro. Cary, I don't think any one could be with him long without being blessed spiritually.

I see that some one will write his life, and that the papers are to be sent to you. Will you write it? or if you don't, R. W. Bigham would give us a good thing, if he will take hold of it.

Some things in regard to our Brother that I would not like to be lost, and for fear that you might not get the information from better hands, I thought I would write to you at once.

If you remember, I was at White Oak the day Brother Willis claimed the blessing of sanctification. Before the service commenced, we had a grove meeting, and on our way back to the church he said to me: "I received something at Richmond camp-ground that I thought was this blessing, but Captain Farris told me I had better mind how I claimed that blessing, for it was high grounds; so I began to doubt, and lost it." I told him that he would have to claim it by faith. I then quoted Rom. vi: 11: "Likewise reckon ye also yourselves to be dead indeed unto sin, but alive unto God through Jesus Christ our Lord." He said: "Why did you not tell me this sooner?"

We went on into the house, and you said, "Brethren, pray for the Holy Spirit," and called on me to pray, and I prayed in my usual stammering, weak way; you preached, and at the close of the services Brother Willis got up and said: "I am going to say something that no human being ever heard me say before. I have received the blessing of sanctification." I remember it distinctly. No wonder you felt the need of the Holy Spirit when it was going to lead to such important results.

Rev. E. M. Whiting, of the South Ga. Conference, was talking with me one day about Bro. W.; he said, "His words seem to have more force to me than any man's I ever heard." I was going from White Oak camp-ground, quite a company of us had gone to Thomson to take the train, and while standing at the depot, Bro. Willis walked up into the crowd and raising his hands, said: "Thou shalt call His name Jesus, for He shall save His people from their sins." I had heard the Scripture often before, and had often read it, but I never saw so much meaning in it before, it seemed to go through and through me.

Soon after the report was circulated in the Charleston papers that he was dead, (this was fifteen years before he died) we were attending a meeting in Augusta, Ga., at St. James, and he said to me: "I want you to go with me this afternoon up to Harrisburg; I started a Sunday-school up there before I went off to Charleston, and I want to go up and see how they are getting on." I told him I would go with him. Directly after we started he proposed that we go up Ellis street, which led us by the livery stables. I soon found he wanted to get to speak to some of those wicked men about their souls. When they saw him I think they tried to get the start of him by asking him questions, and talking so fast that he could not say anything to them; they began thus: "Hey, Miller, we heard you was dead;" to which he replied, "No, sir, I am not dead." "Well, Miller, now if you had your way, hadn't you rather be dead; you know you would be better off; hadn't you rather be in heaven than here; now, really, don't you wish you had died." He stood leaning on his staff, looking at the ground, with his head turned slightly to one side and in deep study for a short while, when he raised his head and looking at the stable-man, he said, "Sir, if the Lord were to place my destiny in my hands, I would hand it right back to him, for fear I would make a mistake."

My Brother, some call him crazy, but could a philosopher have given a better answer, if he had been given hours to prepare it? I trow not. I have thought of that answer many, many times, and that this is the conclusion of the matter: My destiny is in the very best hands that it is possible to place it, hence it would be folly to take it out. Soon after we had passed the stables I proposed that we take the street car, as the weather was very warm and he a cripple. He confessed that he was tired and feeble, but said, "I have been fighting the running of the street cars on Sunday, and now for me to patronize them would be inconsistent." What a rebuke and lesson to me! We walked on up there and found Bro. Tom Gibson conducting a Sunday-school, in a school building (I think) near where St. Luke's church now stands. If we had an omnicient eye to look into the matter, would we not see that Miller Willis helped lay a very important stone in the foundation of St. Luke's church, as well as many others? Yes, for he was a power for good wherever he went. He once told me of a circumstance that occurred in his boyhood days, which shows the faith he had in the efficacy of prayer, even before he was converted. He said, "When I was a boy I took great delight in teasing drunken men; one day I saw a man staggering along the street, I slipped up behind him and caught him by the coat-tail and ginned him around two or three times, and when I turned him loose he fell some distance, with his head doubled up under him, and there he lay motionless; I thought his neck was broken; I ran home and went up stairs, by the side of my bed; I fell down on my knees and begged the Lord not to let that man die, for my mother had often said to me, Miller, you can come home dead but don't come home and tell me you have killed any one."

Several other things that present themselves to my mind, but they are of minor importance, and for fear I may prove tedious, I will close by asking, whom will his mantle fall on?

CHAPTER XIX.

LETTER FROM R. K. MOSELEY TO THE EDITOR.

SEWARD, GA., Sept. 19th, 1891.

REV. W. C. DUNLAP:—I see in the *Wesleyan* that you are to write the life of our dear deceased brother, Miller Willis. I have often thought, since his death, surely some one will write his life; and oh, how I long to see it. It was my good fortune to meet and be with him at two or three camp-meetings in the North Georgia Conference, and I know he was the most Christ-like man I ever met. Some called him a *crank;* I would to God that this old world were filled with such as he; it would be Heaven enough for me. Let the people call him what they will—if he were a crank, then Heaven is full of cranks. I shall never forget his greetings; was it good morning, good evening, or howdy, as is the custom of the day? No, no; he had no respect for the customs of this world where souls were at stake. He had three sorts of salutations, formulated into questions: 1. If a stranger, "How is your soul?" or if an acquaintance, and he knew you professed conversion and sanctification, still it was, "How is your soul to-day?" 2. "Have you been converted?" 3. "Have you been sanctified?" Whatever the answer might be to those questions, his answer was invariably the same: "Well, praise the

Lord!" This was accompanied by the throwing back his head, with his eyes uplifted to Heaven, and the raising of his hand in that way peculiar to himself. I remember once at Pleasant Grove camp-meeting that some one came in and announced that Brother Parks, the Presiding Elder, was sick and could not attend the meeting. Brother Willis cried out: "Well, praise the Lord!" I have seen young men run from him; he would seem to take no notice of them for the moment, even walking the other way, but ere they were aware of it he would be right among them, when they would find it impossible to escape without answering his pointed questions about their souls. I have watched the columns of the *Wesleyan Christian Advocate* since his death, and have read with profound interest some sketches and incidents of his life by Revs. C. C. Cary, George W. Yarbrough, and R. W. Bigham, and it did my very soul good to read the testimony of such men to the character and usefulness of our sainted brother. I do praise God that it was my privilege to meet and be with such a man. While he basks in the smiles of his Redeemer, his work goes on down here.

Oh, for plenty such as he, and soon the strongholds of sin and satan will be torn down, and the kingdom of Heaven built in their stead. Trusting that the Lord will sanctify his life to the conversion of thousands of sinners, as also to the sanctification of believers, I am

Your brother in Christ's love, R. K. MOSELEY.

The following tribute is from the pen of Rev. James L. Ivey, local preacher and pastor in the North Georgia Conference:

S. MILLER WILLIS.

The first time I heard of him was in 1875. Rev. W. W. W—th said in a sermon that "Brother Willis was like a bombshell with a short fuse easy to light, ready to burst in the midst of a crowd, and bound to hit somebody."

So I found him in Sparta, Ga., during the session of the annual conference in the winter of 1876. Rev. J. A. Reynolds preached, Rev. H. C. Christian concluded, and in the midst of the meeting Brother Willis came to me and inquired if I was converted; I replied that I was. I thought he would rejoice to hear my answer, but he seemed to take it as a matter of course, and turning to a crowd of people in the little chapel, exclaimed, "well then, why don't you get to work to have somebody else converted?" He at once passed on and seemed to have selected the hardest case in the house, and soon had him down on his knees crying to God for mercy.

The fact that our sainted brother approached all classes of men in his appeals and warnings does not prove that he was fool-hardy and recklessly bold, for he said sometimes for fear he would be frowned out of countenance and lose courage when ready to speak to the haughty, he would shut his eyes when he began the conversation.

At Norwood a brother said to him during a protracted meeting, "I have always wanted to pray all night, but no one would join me." Brother Willis said, "I will spend the night in prayer with you." And notwithstanding his poor health, he and this brother wrestled in prayer to God until both were about exhausted, and the dawning of the morning was near.

The last time I met him was at a holiness convention. His health was such that he could not attend all the services. We heard of a young minister that had quit our church, and was in league with an unscriptural sect, and he wanted to pay him a visit. When we reached this brother's place of business, he was sent for and made his appearance. Brother Willis plead with him to sever his connection with that party and return once more to our beloved church. We had about eight prayers in all over the matter. Brother Willis, with pale, upturned face and his eyes fixed upon the ceiling, was a correct picture of grief, as he in piteous tones continued to beseech the brother. "Come back! come back! dear brother, or you will be ruined. Little 'B. C.'s' name has been a household word all over Georgia." This young minister afterwards saw his error and returned. Who knows but in answer to the fervent prayers of the holy man of God?

Some of the scripture texts and religious mottoes are kept as mementoes from this good man. The writer found one pinned to the cloth that covered the pulpit board in a rural log church in one of the dark places of

Georgia. Our brother, in some respects, resembled John the Baptist as a forerunner, preparing the way for the coming of his Lord to the hearts of many, long bolted by sin. Like a clap of thunder and a bolt from a clear sky, he would often startle a multitude with his Heaven-heated shot—arouse them from their lethargy and cause them to think as never before.

Truly a prophet has been among us, and his mission was accomplished in our midst.

But his work is over here—not only done, but *well* done. He has received a prophet's reward, and has entered into his Master's joy.

May his mantle fall on some one who is worthy to receive it, that the work of warning may continue until the Lord shall wake a sleeping world.

> "Green grow the turf above thee,
>   Brother of our better days;
> Few knew thee but to love thee,
>   Or named thee but to praise."

JAMES L. IVEY.

Bremen, Ga., Sept. 23, 1891.

LETTER FROM DR. H. V. HARDWICK.

CONYERS, April 30, 1892.

DEAR BRO. DUNLAP:—I write you a few items in the life of our sainted brother Miller Willis that may serve as pointers to the spirit that controlled and led this humble yet wonderful man of God.

I first met him at a country church, where I had driven several miles to meet you, as you will remember, to prevent, if I could, your taking him with you to the church of my membership, where you were soon to begin a protracted meeting, believing, from what I had heard, that Brother Willis would hinder rather than help the meeting. I found you and Brother Willis alone when I drove up. You introduced us and excused yourself leaving us together. I had understood that Brother Willis would not talk of anything but salvation, but to my surprise he entered at once into a very pleasant conversation, referring to having seen me on a former occasion at a crowded church; he spoke of the uncomfortable seats, poor ventilation, sultry weather and suffocating audience. He then branched off on the lack of proper architectural skill in church edifices, and especially country churches, where comfort and convenience and proper ventilation were greatly neglected. I soon found that he could not only talk about matters of general interest, but that he was a man of fine sense. After talking awhile he turned to me and again extending his hand said, "Brother, how is it with your soul?" I said, "All right." "Praise the Lord," said he. "Do you love God with all your heart?" I said, "I hope so." "You must know so, and may the Lord give you the blessing of perfect love." My heart was touched. He rode home with me from church, and before I had reached my front gate he had won my heart—his meekness, simplicity, gentle manners, loving words and sweet spirit, all combined to convince me that he was enjoying a Christian experience that rose above my own; that his life bore a likeness and a relationship to Christ that I had not realized, and my heart began to reach out for the something better and grow hungry for sweeter food. That very night, God, for Christ's sake, let into my heart the white light of divine truth and showed me for the first time my depravity, inbred sin. Oh! how every fiber of body shook and trembled as I looked at my inheritance. The old Adam in my heart. None but the sanctified can understand this fearful revelation and the earnestness of my prayer for cleansing. Brother Willis was by me in this hour of crucifixion, praying, teaching, helping, and when the cleansing power came joined in the hallelujah that echoed back from glory. From that happy hour I was with him much for a time, and frequently in after years. He spent some weeks in my home, and every day was fruitful of blessings to me and my family.

His consecration was so thorough, his faith so perfect and his salvation so full, that he seemed to hold constant communion with God. Yes, it may be said truthfully, he walked with Christ. I have always associated him with the disciple whom Christ loved, St. John, and have no doubt that much that he said was inspired. I saw him approach a prominent lawyer friend of mine on the train—he was a stranger to Brother Willis—and ask him: "Are you a Christian?" His answer was, "I hardly know." "Then," said Brother Willis, "hear what God says about it: 'I would that you were either hot or cold, but since ye are neither hot nor cold, I will spew thee out of my mouth,'" then handing him a tract he left him. I saw that his words had reached the lawyer's heart.

I was walking with him on one occasion along Marietta street, Atlanta, Ga., when turning suddenly aside he confronted two men who were engaged in conversation. Extending his hand to them, he said: "What would become of you if you were to die right now?" One of them said: "We would go to the spirit world." "To what church do you belong?" asked Willis. "We are Spiritualists," one of them answerd. "I knew," said Willis, "the moment my eyes fell on you, that you were deceived by the devil." The other gentleman turned to me and asked: "When did he lose his mind?" Brother Willis heard him, and turning to him quickly, answered: "Twenty-four years ago, and got the mind of Christ—when did you lose yours?" The man was dumb. Then shaking hands with them and expressing his love for them, asked the Lord to save them and passed on, leaving them in fine humor, and no doubt wondering what manner of man he was.

At another time we were riding along and were passing a crowd of convicts in stripes and chains, at work on the street. As we reached the midst of them, Miller Willis shouted to them: "In chains here, how will it be with you hereafter?" Every man dropped his pick and shovel and gazed in silent astonishment at him. While all eyes were bent on him, he lifted his hand above his head and shouted again: "A great many of us who have them not on our legs, have them on our hearts, and if our hearts were exposed we would have them on our legs."

I was attending a certain holiness convention, and heard one morning that Brother Willis was in his room sick. Brother C. and I went over to see him. We found him up and in the front veranda. The hour for morning service was near at hand, and we soon left. After we had passed out the front gate and started down the street, Brother Willis called to us and came hurriedly out and said: "Brethren, I am afraid we have done wrong. Come back and let's have prayer with Brother S. before you go." We went back. He called Brother S. and told him we wanted to pray with him. Brother S. led us into the parlor and knelt by a sofa. Brother Willis knelt by his side and began to talk and pray that Brother S. might receive the blessing of entire sanctification. I noticed a son of Brother S. standing in the hall, and beckoned him in. He knelt for prayer and was converted; and then Sister S. came in and knelt; then another son came in and he, too, was converted. The Holy Ghost came upon Brother S. and his wife and all present, filling the room like unto Pentecost.

I could relate many other like facts and instances that came under my observation, but these will suffice to indicate in some degree the life and character of this the greatest, purest, best man I ever knew. Great in goodness, grand in purity, noble in fidelity, lofty in humility, he laid down a robe of righteousness to put on a crown of glory. H. V. HARDWICK.

CHAPTER XXI.

LETTER TO THE EDITOR FROM BROTHER SAM HUSTER, OF ATHENS, GA.

Rev. W. C. Dunlap:

MY PRECIOUS AND BELOVED BROTHER:—You ask me to write what I know of the life of Miller Willis. I feel that this would be to attempt an impossibility, for no mortal man can express, no pen can describe what I saw, heard, felt and received from the walk and conversation of this godly man. Though he be dead, yet he speaketh. God bless his memory.

I first learned of him through a conversation which I had with Dr. R. W. Bigham, during the first year of his Presiding Eldership at Athens, Ga. He had spoken of the Bible Christian, or the man who walks with God, living a holy life, when I said, "Where is your man?" Brother Bigham replied, "I know of one man whom I believe comes as near that standard as any man that I ever saw." I replied, "Send for him and I will pay his way and will board him a month." He came, and no one can imagine my experience with him, unless they have known him. What a peculiar man he was. The first thing he said to me was the question, "Have you been converted?" I said, "Yes." "Well, have you been sanctified?" I replied, "I don't know." "Well

—that is one thing I would know like it is in 1st Thess. 5:23: 'The very God of peace sanctify you wholly; and I pray God your whole spirit and soul and body be preserved blameless unto the coming of the Lord.'"

My wife and children, with many others, thought him crazy. I thought to myself, "I am in for it, but I invited him to my house, and I must be gentlemanly." The first morning, I asked him to ride down town with me. Every one we met or passed he would say something to, or give them a tract. I felt very much embarrassed when I saw that we would meet the wife and daughter of Col. ———, who were approaching in a carriage. I said, "That is the family of Col. ———; they are 'bon-tons,' don't say anything to them." When just opposite the carriage, he cried out in his peculiarly shrill voice, "What will it profit a man if he gain the whole world, and lose his own soul."

When we reached my office, I said, "Will you go up into my office?" He said, "No, I believe I will walk around and speak a word for Jesus, and drop some of these seeds." He had a bundle of tracts in his hand, and had his long walking stick. He also had with him an old army knapsack made of oil-cloth, which was filled with books and tracts. Among the books was his old, well-worn Bible, and a copy of the Christian's Secret of a Happy Life. He spoke a word or gave a tract to each one he met. Looking up, as he was passing along a side street, he saw a sign with the word "Exchange," and cried out with a loud voice, "what will a man give in exchange for his soul." The bar-keeper, who was a desperate man, and had been known to kick out of his office men who displeased him, called to him, "Hello, when did you get out of the asylum?" Miller Willis, taking no notice of the remark, said, "Is this the place where men exchange their souls for whiskey?" The bar-keeper stepped to the sidewalk, and taking him by the arm, said, "Come in and get a drink." Going inside he found a number of young men, some playing billiards, and others drinking at the bar, to each of whom he gave a tract, and cried out, "There is a young man in this awful place that has a mother in heaven, and he promised to meet her there." Here the bar-keeper interposed, by saying, "Look here, we have had enough of your nonsense, get out." "Well," said Miller, "let us have a word of prayer before I go," and dropping upon his knees, he offered a prayer for the bar-keeper and his customers, such as has rarely ever been heard. The shot went to the mark. A young man followed him out to the side-walk and said, "Who told you?" and he broke down and began weeping. A few nights afterwards he went to church, and as Miller expressed it, "He was sky-blue converted."

The people were soon guying me for having a crazy man as my guest. I said, "All right, some have entertained angels unawares. He is at my house, and it is nobody's business." I spoke better than I knew, for it proved to be better than an angel's visit to me.

Returning home, my wife, seeing that I was perplexed,

inquired: "How do you like your visitor?" I replied, "I have drawn an elephant and do not know what to do with him."

I went with him to Church, and how he did disturb those quiet, highly refined church members, by calling out, "Amen, have faith in God—who is believing?" He would say, "Bless the Lord," and clap his hands as no other man could, until they would pop like a whip. The preacher said, "He may do good in the country, or at some other place, but it will not do at 'The —— Church.'" They did not exactly put him out of the synagogue, but it amounted to almost the same thing.

The preacher in charge of —— church said, "Bring him here and I will turn him loose." What a revival we had. Hallelujah! Seventy-five to a hundred were converted. Many still stand up and say, "That man whom they said was crazy, came along and spoke to me about my soul, and gave me a tract, and it led me to Christ."

Afterwards I went out to the Athens circuit to see more of this man who had stirred up the people like Paul and Silas. I found a large crowd who had been attracted by this wonderful man. People flocked to the altar like doves to the windows, but Miller said that there must be something wrong with the church or else sinners would be converted. He would cry out, "O for faith in God?" "When we get the kind of heart and spirit that David sought and obtained, according to the 51st Psalm, 7th to 10th verse, then sinners will be converted." He would say things that would make persons say, "Somebody has been telling him." He must have been led by the Spirit of God. He had the gift of spiritual discernment in a remarkable degree. He said, "There is division and strife among you." Then brethren that had been at enmity began to make friends, old feuds were settled, the church began to seek such a heart and spirit as David prayed for, and sinners were converted by the score. At a grove prayer-meeting Miller fell down, with his face buried in his hands, and cried out, "Lord, convert a soul now. I will never rise until a soul is converted." I shall never forget my feelings. It made me shudder to hear him say that he would never arise until a soul was converted, but immediately a young man cried out, "O, it is so simple; John can't you see it?" and in a moment his friend responded, "Glory to God," and five or six were converted in a very short time, and we went to the church shouting and praising God. There was no need of preaching that night. It was a time of salvation. The revival spread all over the circuit.

As the time for the meeting of District Conference was near at hand, some of the preachers said that it would not do for Brother Willis to go to that meeting. They said that he would disturb the people. I said, "He claims to be led by the Spirit of God, and if this is true, I will not fight against God." Miller, not knowing anything of this, said, "Well, by the blessing of God, if the way opens up, I will go to ⸺ to the

District Conference, and if we will have faith in God, we can take that town for Jesus." Continuing, he said, "When I was there several years ago, they almost ran me out of town. A young man cursed me, and he was soon taken very sick, and sent for me, saying, 'I want to beg your pardon for what I said to you.' I replied, 'Beg God's pardon,' and I knelt to pray with him, but the young man said it was too late, and he died without hope."

As we started to ———, and had gone but two or three miles from Athens, a black, threatening cloud appeared in the direction that we were going, and I suggested that we had better turn back. Miller replied, "No; when you put your hand to the plow, never look back. Elijah was a man of like passions as we are, and he prayed that it might not rain, and it did not. Let us pray that the cloud go around us." I said, "Well, you pray, and I will see what will come of your faith." We passed on and the cloud went behind us, and we could see as hard a rain as ever I saw, falling within sight of us. Further on I saw another cloud, accompanied with thunder and lightning, and it rained in front of us, but where we were it was dry. As we passed on we soon came to where the water was standing in the road.

When we arrived at ———, Miller, with his long walking stick in hand, and with his tracts, went forth to sow by the wayside. He at once announced that a street meeting would be held on the public square. Some smiled, and others gave looks of diapproval. Some said that it would not do. Miller tried to get help to hold the meeting, and some promised to help him, but when five o'clock, the hour appointed for the meeting, came, some were sick, (?), some had gone to the mill-pond to bathe, and others forgot it (?) until it was too late, but Miller was there, and so was your humble servant. Miller began by crying out "Ho, every one that thirsteth, come ye to the waters," etc. Doctors and lawyers, as well as the street loafers and drunkards, came out to see, they knew not what, but they saw a man full of faith, and of the Holy Ghost. Miller related his religious experience, and then told them that Jesus came to save the worst man in ———.

It then came my turn to speak to the crowd, and pointing to a dilapidated little wooden house down in the hollow, I said, "I took my first drink there. The man that sold it to me is dead and gone." I told them the awful tale of a misspent life, but I said, "God has saved me from a drunkard's grave and a drunkard's hell." Then I plead with them, "O, my friends, will you go on and lose your souls in the end?" I assured them that God would accept what was left of a life that thus far had been misspent. At the close of the meeting almost every man that was present came forward and gave Miller his hand, pledging himself to be a better man, and come to church. A great revival followed. It was said that all but four or five adult persons in the town joined the church.

Miller Willis took a deep interest in my welfare. He prayed for me, and helped me to give up my old habits and my old associates. Once when he came to my house and inquired for me, my wife, who knew better than any one else what it implied, said, "Brother Willis, I am sorry to say it, but he has gone fox hunting." She says that she never heard such a prayer as he offered for me, and that she knew that God would answer that prayer—and He did, for I have never gone since. Several times I tried, but God interfered in some way. Once when I was preparing to go, the feeling came over me that I might be killed in the hunt, and remembering Brother Willis' prayer, I gave up going, and finally becoming convinced that God would answer the prayer at any cost, I gave away my dogs, and gave up my last and most cherished sport—but, glory be to God, I found something better.

Several times after he had come to be almost as one of the family, he would be in some distant place and have an impression that I was overtaken in a fault or had backslidden, and he would write or come to me at once. At one time I thought I would not tell him that I had lost the witness of my sanctification, and I tried to appear cheerful, but he continued to question me, and finally said, "Brother Hunter, you do not ring right; I want to hear you pray like you did once." I said, "Well, God has told you all about it, we will go up stairs and tarry until the Holy Ghost comes and sits as a refiner's fire and makes me ring right."

A certain brother who took a very active part in church work, wanted to get license to preach. Miller went home with him and stayed all night. I asked him afterwards, "What do you think of him?" He replied, "I will tell you how it is. His wife is a one thousand dollar woman tied to a five cent man." His estimate proved to be correct.

He lived by faith. When he needed anything he would ask God. At one time he wanted to go from Athens to Charleston, and after counting his money he found that he lacked $2.50. He prayed, asking the Lord to help him, and then packed his valise and started to the train. On his way he met Col. ——, a banker, who said to him, "My friend, I thought you might be in need of some money, will you accept this?" It was the exact amount he needed to take him to Charleston.

He never asked any one for anything, and if more was given him than he had immediate need of, he would give it away, or spend it for some good books, or for tracts for distribution.

Men who thought when he first came to Athens, that he ought to be sent to the insane asylum, soon found that he was wise in the things of God, and were glad to invite him to their homes and to ask him to pray for themselves and for their families. There are hundreds of men and women in the land who have it to say, "Miller Willis said something to me which awakened me, and brought me to Christ."

Once while he was at my house he had a hemorrhage from the lungs, and I thought he was gone, but he revived, whispering "Amen, if God has more use for me in heaven than on earth, Amen—Glory to Jesus."

It is hard now for me to feel that he is dead. He is not dead; he has entered into life. As he passed away I lost a precious friend on earth; was made poorer, but heaven richer. S. M. HUNTER.

Here is the last letter he ever wrote Brother Hunter:

"Have faith in God, Mark xi: 22, 23, 24; praise God! January 10th, 1891. Did you hear that, beloved? and what is the best thing you have to say of Jesus this morning? I say, 'Truly God is good to Israel, even to such as are of a clean heart.'

"Oh, hallelujah to God! Brother Hunter! I don't know where to begin nor where to end, for surely Psalm 23: 'The Lord is my shepherd and I shall not want. He maketh me to lie down in green pastures; he leadeth me beside the still waters.'

"I have never been out to but one meeting since I have been here at Duke, but my faith is, *I shall not die, but live and preach the gospel.*

"Does Pierce still pray for me? Tell Scott I want her to be mighty smart, if I live to get back to Athens.

"Brother Hunter, can you say to-day, as you told me when I left—'Brother Willis, my heart is just right, and

I am wrapped up in the thirteenth chapter of first Corinthians?' Your less than the least, 1st Thess. v: 23,

S. MILLER WILLIS."

INSCRIBED TO MILLER WILLIS BY ONE WHO LOVED HIM.

The blessed Word of God assures us that "The righteous shall be in everlasting remembrance."

Thus their acts, words and spirit remain as precious legacies to their friends and the world.

Such was our dear departed brother. Many will, in the eternal day, rise up and call him blessed. His work on earth was accompanied by the Divine Spirit, and he was the honored instrument of leading many to the Cross of Christ. He resorted to many methods to lead his fellow-men to Jesus.

> "And as a bird each fond endearment tries,
> To tempt its new-fledged offspring to the skies,
> He tried each art, reproved each dull delay,
> Allured to brighter worlds and led the way."

He is one of the characters that stand upon the plains of history; against time past as a background, they seem like silver shafts of beauty—land-marks by which spiritual mariners may steer in the voyage of life, each a Pharos on the jutting headlands of truth. Miller Willis was the most untiring, persevering, and laborious Christian I ever knew. The seed he scattered are growing to-day in many hearts and lives, and are kept fresh by waterings from the same fountain at which he obtained his supply. Many will shine as stars in the crown of his rejoicing forever!

> "After years of earnest battle,
>   Throbbing nerve and heart and soul,
> In the midst of life's wild rattle,
>   July fifteen God called his roll.
> Miller Willis grandly answered,
>   Standing out among the blest:
> 'I was fighting for the Master—
>   Now I'm ready for my rest.'"

CHAPTER XXII.

FROM ROBERT M. ADAM, HIS BROTHER-IN-LAW.

He was converted to God in 1864, after a long struggle and thorough sifting; the question being squarely put as to his willingness to be called crazy or a fool for Christ's sake. He was first aroused to a sense of his peril at the second battle of Manasses, Virginia, but forgot it, and on his return home he attended a meeting, then being conducted in old St. John church, Augusta, Ga., by the pastor, Rev. George G. N. McDonald. On hearing the preacher quote Psalm 1: 14: "Pay thy vows," Miller said it seemed to him it was specially intended for him, and particularly so when he asked if there were not some in the congregation who had vowed to God on battlefields and had failed to perform them. He was thoroughly aroused, and struggled for days through repentance, as one sin after another was brought to his attention, and the final test was made when he was confronted with a full surrender to be called a fool or crazy for Christ's sake. On visiting a relative in the neighborhood one evening, as he was returning home, he resolved on reaching there to go behind the stable, which stood near the line fence between the adjoining lots, with space enough to admit one person, and there remain until he should be blessed or die. When he reached the sidewalk, and near an old mulberry tree, he received the witness of his acceptance with God and went running home to tell his mother the good news. 'Twas then about 10 o'clock, and he went about the neighborhood knocking up the neighbors, telling them of his conversion. He slept very little that night, and the next day he published the news all over the city. Very few believed him, and thought he was playing off. Finally it was thought that it was simply excitement occasioned by the revival meeting, and would soon wear off. Some predicted it would last a week, month, etc., and finally some thought him crazy, and it was freely talked over the city. It came to his ears, and he forgot his promise to God to be willing to be called crazy and so allowed his zeal to flag, and hence lost the joy of salvation. Becoming concerned about his condition, he sought the counsel of Brother James E. Evans, who diagnosed his case, and asked him if he obeyed the leading of the Spirit when directed to talk to people about the salvation of their souls? He said, "Yes, I know now what's the matter," and resolved to be faithful even at the cost of being called crazy; we all know how truly he kept that vow.

At the close of the war he engaged in the grain business with Mr. John Keener, in Augusta. He continued about one year; afterward he kept a wood yard for a year or two. He then gave up business in the main, helping me in mine, as it suited him, I having married his sister in 1866, and he having come to live with us. His time even then was wholly given up to Christian work, he doing all he could to extend his Redeemer's kingdom by holding prayer-meetings in different parts of the city. In 1867, I was converted and early joined him in the good work. He was often called to visit the sick and administer to the dying. In 1874, when I removed with my family to Charleston, S. C., the Y. M. C. A. of Augusta offered him a salary to remain and continue in the work. This he did for a time, but it was not to his liking. Miller Willis was thoroughly Arminian. As every one knows, the Y. M. C. A. is a mixture of all denominations. While he had great love and respect for these brethren individually, and rejoiced in all the good done by them in their non-denominational work, yet, for him, there was only one course to pursue, and that was to put the truth straight as he believed it, at all times and everywhere. From this time he gave himself in all his work to the promulgation of radical Christianity in accordance with what he believed to be the teachings of the scriptures and the Methodist Church. At our earnest entreaty he came to Charleston and made his home with us for several years, except as he made occasional visits back to Georgia to help ministers, who would write for him, in revival labors. He contracted the habit of chewing and smoking when a boy, and became a most inveterate user of the weed, often smoking and chewing at the same time. He quit chewing, after a hard struggle, in 1868-9, and later on gave up smoking. When resolved on duty he never hesitated or drew back.

During a union revival service, held in Charleston, S. C., at a morning meeting, when an opportunity was given for experience, a Presbyterian pastor of one of the churches arose and told of a young man who had been converted the day previous, and said he had told him that now he was all right, and that, while he might fall away, he would always come back. Being present myself, and knowing Miller, I watched him to see what he would do. As the Brother made the remark concerning the final perseverance of his young friend, Miller reached forward, and with his hands on the pew in front of him, watched the Brother closely, and as soon as he started to sit down, Miller pulled himself up quickly, before the Brother had gotten seated, and quoted Ezek. 18-24, and sat down. The impression was profound.

In a revival at Trinity church, Charleston, the pastor took occasion to say one evening that, in case any one desired to see him about their souls, his office hours were thus and so, and he would be glad to have them call; before he finished the sentence Miller called out, "Well, praise God, the Lord Jesus is in His office all the time; you'll have no trouble finding Him."

When he first went to Charleston, a gentleman of my acquaintance stopped me one day on the street and asked who my friend was. After having him describe the man, I told him he was a friend of mine from Georgia.

I inquired why he asked about him. "Well," he said, "is there not something wrong with him?" I said I didn't think so, and urged him to stop him sometime and have a talk with him; but he laughed and declined, saying, "Well, he did a very strange thing the other day." "And what was that?" "Well, he was passing the store, it was crowded with customers, he stepped into the door and, lifting up his hand, called out in a loud voice, 'What shall it profit a man if he shall gain the whole world, and lose his own soul?'" "I am glad you remember it, for I have no doubt you have often heard it from the pulpit and forgotten it." He was certainly the most faithful and fearless witness for God I ever knew. On Sunday, when street cars or other vehicles used for pleasure or business would pass him, he would call out, "Remember the Sabbath day," etc.

He was called to see a brother in Charleston who had met with an accident, and broken his thigh or hip bone, and the doctors were setting it. During the operation, which was accompanied with excruciating pain, Miller sympathized with him so deeply that it seemed to the physician who related the circumstance to me, that he felt the pain, and would cry out as if enduring the agony with and for his friend. Indeed, he seemed to bear it for him, without which, the physicians declared, it appeared impossible for his friend to have survived the painful operation. He was an excellent nurse, and could quiet and soothe a nervous person in a most remarkable manner. He was particularly expert with children, possessing all the sympathy and tenderness of christian womanhood, with a remarkable charm in controlling them.

My mother died when I was five years old; at the age of seven I was taken by my elder brother, together with a brother eighteen months older than myself, to Mr. S. M. Thompson's to board. Mrs. Thompson was an aunt of Miller's, so that by this providence I became early associated with him; indeed, one might say we grew up together. He was about twelve years old when I first knew him. He was my senior by a few years, and this gave him, naturally, an influence over me; besides he rather took us under his protection, and ofttimes saved us from the oppression of other boys, and, I am sorry to say, taught us much mischief and vice, by precept and example. I have never known or heard of worse boys than those who lived in Augusta, Ga., at that time, and among the "chief of sinners" was Miller Willis, the leader and captain in every daring and desperate undertaking, from a pitch battle with rocks and brickbats to scaling high walls, or swimming the Savannah river. There were no police in the city at that time, and we were unrestrained in a great measure. Fighting was an every-day and general occurrence among boys, and often for very trivial offenses, and sometimes without cause. Miller was an aggressive fellow, constantly stirring up strife among others, in which he frequently took a hand. When he was about I felt quite safe from the attacks of my enemies, and was often stimulated to attack them, feeling assured of a strong backing and fair play. During the summer season, many Augusta boys used to cross the river, going to swim at Brooks' millpond, about two and a half miles away. Passing through Hamburg, S. C., we were sometimes set upon by boys who lived there. We determined to punish them if possible, and arranged for a regular pitched battle; Miller was the leader of the Augusta boys. He and his brother, Milton, had two goats, a large one that they trained to pull, and a smaller one to push a small wagon, and with this team, we hauled stones and brickbats for several days to the bridge, and when all was in readiness, the boys assembled on both sides of the river. There were a hundred or more in either party. Arming ourselves with stones, we were led across the bridge by our commander. As soon as we landed on the Carolina side, we were vigorously met, and so the fight opened. From about three p. m., until after dark, every inch of ground was hotly contested. Many boys on both sides were seriously injured. The Augusta boys, led on by the intrepid Miller, were finally victorious. He was the "lion of the day." He was an athlete and gymnast. He was known as the most active boy in the city. An expert swimmer, on several occasions, at the peril of his own life, he rescued boys from drowning.

Boys generally were afraid of him and would avoid him, if not on intimate terms with him. While he was a fighter, and always promoted it among boys, he would see fair play and take sides with the weak. Being bold and courageous, even daring, with large combativeness, he was an intrepid leader, always found in the forefront. We sometimes played "Follow your leader," and he as leader would climb up and down dangerous places, one of which was the cliffs near Hamburg. They had been made very precipitous by the railroad company taking earth from the hillsides so that it was nearly forty feet high. Buildings in course of construction were favorite resorts for this purpose, and we thought little of our perilous positions. So the boys followed him into all manner of danger and wrong-doing.

Volumes might be written of his daring exploits, evil deeds and pernicious influence, for his presence was an evil omen. Often might be heard remarks from negroes like this: "Yonder come dem deblish white boys," and they would get out of the way, for they often suffered from his practical jokes and rough handling. They would sometimes report him to his father who would punish him severely, but to no purpose, except it might be to nerve him to revenge at the first opportunity. No one seemed to feel safe when he and his companions were about.

The object in view in writing particularly of his boyhood and life previous to his conversion, is to bring out clearly his aggressive character, which, under God, became a burning zeal for the salvation of souls, and made him the most notable character in this generation, if not in this century, within our knowledge, throughout this section. For, transformed as he was, from a persecutor and pest, to the converted and sanctified defender and promoter of the Faith, he impressed all with his devotion to God.

I praise God for the powerful influence he exerted over me for good; the extent of which eternity alone will reveal.

My intimate association with him—having married his only sister, and our house being his home up to his death—there was no one who knew him so intimately as I. Having been converted myself soon after he was, and helped by him to a decision of a choice of the Methodist church, we were in full sympathy and one in our purpose to serve God and make our way to heaven and carry as many with us as possible.

As we would plan work for the Master, and labor to execute it, his undaunted courage would stimulate me to greater effort. I often remonstrated with him for what I considered his indiscretion until I became thoroughly convinced that he was being directed by the Holy Ghost, and would lead to victory and conquest, and rescue perishing souls from the mighty grasp of satan and sin. I then ceased interposing any objections, and sought to influence others to the same course.

At one time he was alarmed by the sudden death of quite a number of persons he had warned faithfully and for their last time, and so said to me, "I'm afraid now to talk to people about their soul's salvation for fear they will not accept Christ, and will be suddenly destroyed."

About this time he was passing along the street one day, and heard an old man, Mr. M——, an acquaintance of his from his boyhood, swearing fearfully at some one, and he approached him, and, touching him on the shoulder, said: "Swear not at all." The man turned on him, cursed and swore at him in a most blasphemous manner; but Miller paid no attention, and quietly walked away. A short time afterwards Mr. M—— sent for him and told him he wanted to apologize for his behavior to him. Miller told him he had not offended him, but he recalled the circumstances and insisted on apologizing. Miller impressed him with the importance of seeking pardon from God, whose law he had broken, and before leaving him prayed with and for him. This led to his conversion, and within three months Mr. M—— died. Many of Miller's friends, when they heard of his having approached Mr. M—— and rebuked him for swearing, remonstrated with him, and tried to impress him with the impropriety of his course, when one was in such a rage, and that he should have waited for an opportunity after it was passed. But Miller insisted he was led of the Spirit, and the sequel proved it most conclusively.

While on a visit to Athens, Ga., some years since, he was passing a bar-room, and the proprietor, with a number of other men, was standing or sitting on the street in front; they stopped him and the proprietor invited him in; Miller replied that he would go in if he would let him have a prayer-meeting in there, to which they consented, and the proprietor said, "Come in, boys; Miller's going to have a prayer-meeting inside." They all went in. Several young men were inside playing cards. Miller sang and prayed, read a portion of scripture, and gave them a talk. Turning to the young men who were seated at the table, playing cards, he said: "Which one of you young men promised your mother on a deathbed that you would meet her in Heaven? and how are you living?" While he did not know this was a fact, it proved to be so, and one of them reformed.

As he was about to conclude the services, he started to announce that there would be another meeting there the following day, but the barkeeper objected, and told him quietly that he did not think it was a good place to hold such a meeting, and was glad to be rid of him.

On one occasion he saw an old gentleman in Charleston come out of a bar-room wiping his mouth with his handkerchief. He went to him and looking at him said, "Prepare to meet thy God." The old man spoke very shortly to him and told him to go away and not bother him. Some days after the old gent met Major Willis and asked him where his brother was, and said, "That fellow bothers me everywhere I go. Whether on the street cars (he was president of the street car company) or attending to other business, I hear those words ringing in my ears, 'Prepare to meet thy God.' Send him to me, I want to see him." When he called on Mr. C. he gave him five dollars and told him to use it in his work, and any time he wanted more to come to him.

He had a similar experience with some gamblers, who

invited him into their rooms and offered to lend him money to take a hand in their game. Declining, he told them of his wicked life, and urged them to become Christians. After praying with them he left. Some days after they met the Major and requested him to send Miller around to see them. And on going they gave him twenty dollars to use in his work as he pleased. He told them that he had just been asking God to give him ten dollars for a special purpose, and that he wanted them to come with him and see what he wanted with the money, and took them to a poor widow's house, who was in distress, and left the money. The gamblers insisted that he should come to them whenever he needed any help for his work.

When on his way down to my office one morning, in Charleston, having only fifteen cents in his pocket, the Spirit moved him to call at the home of a poor widow and leave the amount with her. But the devil said no, don't do that; but wait until you have more, then go around and give her something that will help her; this fifteen cents won't do any good. But being satisfied it was God's will he should go, he went immediately, and on making the object of his visit known, the poor widow said: "Well, Brother Willis, I have just been asking the Lord to send me fifteen cents to buy a little trimming for my daughter's hat, that she may go to Sunday-school to-morrow."

Miller was always actively engaged in Christian work, and when he was impressed to take up any work, or open new enterprises for God, he might ask some one to help, but whether he had helpers or not, he was never deterred. Before leaving Augusta for Charleston, he established a Sunday-school in the suburbs at Harrisburg, near a place of resort for gamblers and men who fought chickens and dogs on Sundays. He had a prayer-meeting there during the week, and was always found at his post, pushing the work; so that the sporting characters were annoyed and forced to abandon their place of rendezvous; but not before making an effort to break up his meetings. He paid no attention to them, and was not aware that they had violated the law by attempting to disturb the meetings, for which they were indicted and fined, and half of the amount was paid to him to carry on his work. St. Luke's church, Augusta, is likely the result of his labors in that vicinity.

When living in Charleston he was impressed to go out on Sunday afternoons on the battery and hold a street meeting, as crowds generally promenaded there at that time. He was finally stopped by a policeman, who threatened to take him in if he did not desist. He said to him that of course he would be subject to the powers that be and stop if they insisted. Later he obtained permission from the mayor to hold an open air meeting, and determined on having it at the post office during the hours when mail was delivered on Sunday, about one o'clock. He was interrupted there one Sunday by a policeman and ordered to desist, but there were quite a number there who insisted that he should not be interfered with. On telling me of the circumstances, I said I would accompany him on the following Sunday. I had long been impressed that I ought to assist him in this work, and even felt it would be cowardly not to do so; yet, when attending the meeting with him the following Sunday, I failed to stand with him, but remained on the opposite side of the street, for which I was heartily ashamed, and ever after stood with him and assisted in the services. Sometime afterwards the Lord called Brother Thos. H. Leitch to help us, and although he came very reluctantly at first, he was faithful and continued the work after we left Charleston, and I believe that work has been continued by some one ever since. And thus it has often been the mission of our dear departed brother to pioneer work for God.

He was my constant companion when at Charleston, and when not otherwise engaged was in my office during the day. We often conferred together on matters of business, and I found him a wise counselor, being quick of perception and a good judge of human nature. We sized those with whom I had dealings; and in time of depression and doubt, as to proper course to pursue, we would retire to a private room and lay the matter before our God and ask Him to help and guide. After meeting with heavy losses and reverses in business, God opened the way for me to a new business, which I started in a very small way and soon found I needed capital and a more convenient place to manufacture in. I made a proposition to a neighbor and brother Methodist to join me and furnish the capital, which he agreed to do, and was to receive half the profits. He soon found it was a very profitable business and wanted to push me out, giving me only a trifle. This was a very trying time, for I needed money sadly and was just getting on my feet. We prayed much over this, and finally decided to stop the supply of chemicals that were being shipped to Charleston on my order to my partner; this accomplished, it would force him to my terms. A supply was needed to carry on the work, and it was on board a steamer then lying in dock, just arrived from New York. I wired to the shippers and just as the barrels were discharged from the steamer and were about to be loaded on to a dray (for the goods were needed badly to supply pressing orders in hand) the boy presented a telegram ordering the steamer agent to deliver the goods to me instead of party to whom they were shipped. This brought my partner to terms and settlement was agreed upon; Miller Willis' great tact, amounting almost to a charm.

We had hoped to have him home with us more than he seemed to think he could be and continue in the line of duty; so that he had not been with us for three years, when he returned for the last time, although he had intended coming at least a year before; but he became engaged in work and was thus prevented. How we all longed to have him with us, and then when he did get home my circumstances were such that I could not be there to welcome him, and was unable to be with him but a few days of the time. My wife, his devoted sister, and our dear children, were untiring in their attentions—doing all in their power for his relief and comfort. During all his suffering not a murmur of complaint escaped his lips, and he was always perfectly resigned to God's will, saying if God had no more active work for him to do, his desire was that He would take him home. When asked by his sister why he wanted to go and leave them, he replied: "Well, I'm ready now, but can't tell how it might be with me later."

I was notified by telegram of his extreme illness, and my prayer was that I might be permitted to attend him in his last hours and hear his last words. On reaching home the afternoon before his death, I found him sinking rapidly. He could not turn himself in bed, and he recognized my voice, and I said to him: "Trusting Jesus?" and he added: "*That's all.*"

It was difficult to persuade him to take any nourishment, and his sister suggested that we try to get him to take a little blackberry wine some friend had sent him, and I poured about a tablespoonful on a little cracked ice, but he could not be induced to take it. As he wanted some ice we poured the wine off and gave him a piece, but as soon as he tasted it and discovered it had been in the wine he spit it out. I asked him if he wanted me to sing for him, and he said, sing the "New Song," and I sang the one I knew in "Joy and Gladness" collection, and when through, he said, "Sing the other one," but I did not know it then. The one he wished sung was that in Brother Charlie Tillman's collection. "Wait a Little While then We'll Sing the New Song." His brother, Maj. E. Willis, came a on train an hour or so after I arrived, and finding my wife weary and worn by her constant attentions to him, we did all we could to relieve her but with little effect, as she was anxious to know his every wish and do everything possible for his comfort. I had succeeded in quieting her and went into Brother Miller's room about 6:30 a. m., and found him nearing the end. His limbs were cold; his eyes seemed fixed, and although open, he could not see. I knelt by his side and said: "Trusting Jesus!" he replied, "that's all." To which I replied, "Praise the Lord," and he said, "Amen! Amen!" I then asked if he were in any pain, he answered, "No." "Well, praise the Lord," I said, and he replied, "Amen! Amen! do you hear me?" "Yes; are you still trusting Jesus?" "*Now* and *forever!* Amen! Amen! do you hear me? do you hear me?" I called to the Major to know if he heard him, and he did. He had been breathing with some effort, but now began to breathe at longer intervals, and I called to Major to come quickly, he was going, and he reached him in time to see him expire, and without a struggle. This all occurred within about five minutes, and, as he called back to know if I heard him, he appeared to call from a distance loud enough to be heard in the adjoining room. It seemed he had crossed over and was calling back to say "it was well with him—safe at Home, and to be forever with Jesus our adorable Lord." "Trusting Jesus *now* and *forever!*"

"Praise God from whom all blessings flow." "His praise shall continually be in my mouth," for the blessed privilege of sweet communion and fellowship, with the saint of God, S. Miller Willis.

CHAPTER XXIII.

FUNERAL SERVICE IN HONOR OF BROTHER MILLER WILLIS AT ST. JAMES' CHURCH, AUGUSTA, GA., JULY 16TH, 4 O'CLOCK P. M.

"The casket was placed in the auditorium of St. James, Wednesday night, July 15th, by a number of ministers and laymen, who received it at the Augusta depot, from Spartanburg. Maj. Willis and Brother Adams (brother and brother-in-law of deceased), accompanied the remains from Spartanburg. Throughout the day (Thursday) many friends and christian brethren of Brother Willis visited the church to pay their respects to his remains. The Methodist pastors and Brother Rees, from Watkinsville, took part in the funeral service. Brother Rees read first, hymn No. 599; Brother Dunlap, of Asbury, offered the prayer; Brother Timmons, of St. Luke, read first lesson; Brother Wadsworth, of St. John's, read second lesson; the pastor of St. James delivered the sermon from I. Cor. xv:58; Brother Frazer, of Broad Street, read second hymn, No. 647, with refrain—

"Home, home, sweet, sweet home."

The audience filled the large church, and a long procession followed the casket to the grave. There were in the audience and procession representatives of the different denominations of the city. At the grave Brother Dunlap read the service, and Brother Timmons pronounced the benediction. Throughout, it was an occasion of triumph and rapture rather than sadness and gloom.

As I stated, in a private note to Brother C. C. Cary, death seemed to have been whipped away from the very body of the good man, so natural did the face appear, and the angels seemed to be caressing it.

"Praise God from whom all blessings flow,"

Was sung by request, just before the benediction was pronounced, and the good brethren and sisters kept up the sweet songs as long as they lingered about the grave.

The grave was beautifully decorated with choice flowers, Brother Miller's favorite exhortation, "Have faith in God," having been woven into a wreath, and placed at the head of the grave.

Large as was the attendance at the funeral service, many could not attend, and the following memorial service was arranged for the next Sunday evening:

PROGRAMME OF MILLER WILLIS' MEMORIAL SERVICE AT ST. JAMES, AUGUSTA, GA., JULY 19TH, 8:15 P. M., 1891.

First hymn, No. 407.
Prayer—By Rev. W. A. Rodgers.

SCRIPTURAL READINGS.

1. By Mrs. Plank—Gen. v:24.
2. By Mrs. Sherman—Ps. xii:1.
3. By Brother Stubbs—Eph. iii:14–21.

4. By Brother Sherman, Sr.—Matt. ——.
5. By Brother Lester—I. Thess. v:23.
6. By Brother Jones—I. John iii:1–3.
7. By Brother Parks—Matt. v:16.
8. By Brother Baggett—John iii:16.
9. By Pastor—"This man receiveth sinners."
10. By Rev. W. A. Rodgers—Rev. xxii:1–7.
Second hymn, No. 411.
1. Tribute from Mrs. W. C. Sibley, of the Presbyterian church—read by the pastor.
2. Tribute from Rev. C. C. Cary—read by the pastor.
3. Sketch of life—By Dr. Eugene Foster.
Third hymn, No. 415.
4. Tribute by Brother John Weigle.
5. Tribute by Brother Josiah Miller.
Fourth hymn, No. 356.
6. Tribute by Brother Wm. Parks.
7. Tribute by Prof. Sheeut, of Baptist church.
8. Tribute by Brother Adam, of Spartanburg, S. C.
Last hymn, No. 918.
Benediction—By Rev. W. A. Rodgers.
(Methodist Hymn and Tune Book used).

From The Augusta Chronicle:

"As life was ebbing away," Mr. Adams said, "I leaned over him and asked, 'Are you trusting in Jesus?' He replied, 'That's all.'

"I said, 'Praise the Lord.' He answered, 'Amen.'

"He was cold and his eyes were almost set. He could

not see me, but he could hear my voice and understand me. 'Are you in pain?' I asked. 'No.'

"'Praise the Lord for that,' I said, and again he answered, 'Amen.'

"'Are you still trusting to Jesus?'

"'Now and forever,' he replied; and then he asked: 'Do you hear me?'

"'Yes, praise the Lord,' I said, and with 'Amen' on his lips he died. It seemed to me that when he asked if I heard him, his spirit had already crossed over the river, and, standing on the shores of Paradise, he called back to know if I could hear his last testimony for Christ."

REMARKS.

Early in the evening the people began to assemble, and by 8:15, time appointed for service to begin, the large auditorium of St. James' church was filled.

Stillness, reverence, and awe rested upon the multitude throughout the service, which lasted two hours.

No crape was used. In its place two vases of beautiful and fragrant flowers adorned the pulpit.

Blessings came upon us all through that service which we cannot outlive.

Augusta, Ga."   GEO. W. YARBROUGH.

From Evening News, July 16, 1891.

MILLER WILLIS.

His Funeral this Afternoon Down at St. James' Church—A Notable and Peculiar Man and What People Say About Him—The Pall Bearers at His Funeral—A Memorial Service.

Miller Willis was the best known man in Georgia among all classes of people.

This is what a man who knew him well said to the *Evening News* to-day, and it is true. He has been all over Georgia and Carolina, and among all sorts of people, and he made a deep impression everywhere he was seen and heard.

Everybody who read last evening about his death had a good word to say about Miller Willis. No man has been found to say aught against him. And yet in life he was called a crank.

He will be buried from St. James' Church at 4:30 o'clock this afternoon. Augusta was his home, or rather his headquarters, and St. James was his church. He worshipped, however, as he worked, everywhere, and the good he has done is beyond calculation. He was never ordained a preacher, and yet he was a better preacher than the majority and more effective than nine-tenths of the preachers of the day.

He was an evangelist ordained by his God, and he looked entirely to his Father, not only for guidance but for His care.

"He was the only man I ever saw who did implicitly and entirely trust in God," said the same friend to-day, one who knew him best, perhaps, and whose home was Miller Willis' headquarters in this city. Continuing, he said: "I have often seen men who said they trusted in the Lord, but Miller Willis is the only one who actually did it all the time. He never worked for money and went about without it, and yet when it was needed to pay his way there was the money. Money seemed to turn up in plenty for him when it was needed, and he never bothered about it. One day I asked him how he was going to get to Athens, his destination, when I knew he only had $2 in his pocket. He replied that he was going to start, and if the Lord did not want him to go any further than $2 would carry him, it was all right, but the money would come. And sure enough a brother, in shaking hands with him a little later, left the needed $3 in Miller's hand."

"His trust and its unfailing supply was shown in another instance. He declared one day that he was going to Spartanburg the next morning, and I knew he had no money at all. 'It will come all right,' said Miller, who was stopping at my house, and sure enough that evening a friend met me and asked me to hand a package to Miller Willis. The friend knew nothing of the proposed trip and I did not think about the contents of the package at the time, but when Miller opened it that night it contained $23. That's what his faith did for him, and it was unfailing. That's the way he lived and he never knew want. He had a wealthy brother who was ready to aid him always and was anxious for Miller to live with his family in Charleston, but the evangelist preferred to do his Master's work in his own way."

Said the same friend: "People used to call Miller Willis a crank, and he did not care. 'It is better so,' he used to say to me, 'for if they think me a crank they will take all I give them, and I give them all the Lord sends.' But the public never made a greater mistake. He would hear the hard things said of him on the street, and would often smile as he told them to me. I never saw him ruffled in my life, and that is more than I can say of the preachers themselves. His life was absolutely pure and perfect, and he may have been peculiar, even cranky, in his manner, but I never enjoyed better company than when he would come to my house. He could talk intelligently and entertainingly on any subject, and often did so, although his best loved theme was religion. Often he would get on the floor and play for hours with my children, and he enjoyed that, too. He was a man, every inch of him, but so earnest in his Christian and evangelistic life, that his persistent talking and working for Christ caused him to be called a crank. He called God his Father and trusted Him, and that is why he got along so well. 'My Father is rich,' he would say, 'and owns the sheep on a thousand hills. Do you suppose He will allow His son to suffer or hunger when He owns so many cattle?' And this is the secret of the life of Miller Willis."

THE FUNERAL THIS AFTERNOON.

The remains of Miller Willis were brought to Augusta from Spartanburg last night by his brother, Major Ed. Willis, and his brother-in-law, Mr. R. N. Adam, and the funeral this afternoon will be attended by a large crowd. The pall bearers will be from the Methodist churches of the city, as follows:

From St. James Church—Messrs. Josiah Miller, Eugene Foster and F. M. Stulb. From St. John's Church —Messrs. Geo. Adam and W. M. Dunbar. From Asbury Church—Mr. J. E. Duren. From St. Luke's Church—Mr. W. O. Bohler. From Broad St. Church —Mr. J. H. Fearey.

All Methodist pastors and other ministers in the city are invited to attend as honorary pall bearers.

A MEMORIAL SERVICE.

Next Sunday night a special service will be held in St. James' Church in Memory of Miller Willis.

[From Augusta Chronicle, July 16, 1891.]

MILLER WILLIS DEAD.

A NOTABLE CHARACTER DIES YESTERDAY IN SPARTANBURG, S. C.

A REMARKABLE EVANGELIST.

THE END OF A LIFE WHICH WAS UNIQUE IN ITS SINGULAR INDIVIDUALITY—THE FUNERAL TO TAKE PLACE THIS AFTERNOON FROM ST. JAMES METHODIST CHURCH.

When Miller Willis died yesterday in Spartanburg, S. C., there passed from earthly life into eternal life one of the most unique characters of this generation.

He died of consumption, at the home of his sister, Mrs. R. M. Adam, of Spartanburg, and the news was received in Augusta yesterday with sadness by many intimate friends of the dead man.

Miller Willis was born in Augusta about fifty years ago. He grew up a mischievous, fun-loving fellow, and was what is commonly termed "one of the boys." He served gallantly through the war, and was the life of many a gathering around the camp fire. It was not until after this that he became connected with the church, and began a new life—the life which has made him notable among men.

Miller Willis was never an ordained minister, but he went about preaching the Gospel to every creature. Short in statue, his hair silvered, he walked constantly with a long staff, such as tourists cut in climbing mountains, and was everywhere a unique and notable personage.

He was never ashamed to speak out for Christ in any assemblage, and he has distributed enough tracts to load a railroad train. He was a roving evangelist, going where the Spirit moved him; frequently without any idea when he started, where he would stop, or how long he would remain. He took no heed of money or expenses, but somehow the

MONEY WAS ALWAYS FURNISHED

from some source whenever he needed it. "The Lord will provide," was his answer to all questions on such subjects. He never lost an opportunity in any crowd, large or small, to say something about Christ and salvation. On entering a railroad car he would cry out to the passengers, "Prepare to meet thy God."

Frequently he would pass through the train, quoting passages of Scripture or making epigrammatic exhortations. Sometimes he entered a car and took his seat without a word, and when all was quiet, would suddenly ejaculate some verse of Scripture containing a warning or a promise.

A MEMORABLE INCIDENT.

One day he chanced to be near the scene of a homicide. A crowd was gathered about the prostrate body of the dead man. Suddenly the patriarchal figure of an unknown man with a long staff appeared in their midst.

Raising his hand aloft, he cried out to the astonished crowd: "Prepare to meet thy God." He disappeared, without another word, as suddenly as he had come among them, but it is safe to say no man in the crowd ever heard a sermon whose lesson he remembers with more distinctness than he does that thrilling incident.

Most people who didn't know him called Miller Willis a crank, but however much one might differ with his methods, no one who ever knew him doubted his goodness of heart, his purity of life, his entire consecration to his work, and his sublime faith in the truth of what he preached.

RECORD OF HIS CONVERSION.

His Bible, which is filled with marginal notes, contains the following interesting entry in his own handwriting:

S. M. Willis was born into the kingdom of God, 1864. He got Matthew xviii: 43 in Augusta, Ga.; was converted, and he knew it, and I know it now, twenty-two years afterwards. To God be all the glory. Was sanctified like 1st Thess. 5 and 23, October 6, 1877, while Brother W. C. Dunlap was preaching from Ephesians iii: 16 to 21.

Now, oh my Jesus, let me say. Kept by the power of God through faith until I go to Heaven for Jesus' sake. Amen. Athens, Ga., July 14, 1866.

Read over. 30: "Knows" in Epistle of John.

He was a great believer in tracts, and besides distributing millions of them, he wrote a great many. He had considerable talent for putting things in striking and epigrammatic style. The following skeleton of a sermon prepared by him is a notable example of this:

REV. MILLER WILLIS' SERMON.

Below we give a synopsis of a sermon prepared by Rev. Miller Willis:

WHICH ROUTE WILL YOU TAKE?

GREAT SALVATION RAILROAD.
FROM
EARTH TO HEAVEN.
Scenery Unsurpassed.
Via
Mount Calvary, the River of Life, Paradise Garden, the High Rock, etc.
Through the Valley of the Shadow of Death.
BY DAYLIGHT.
To the Grand Central Depot of the Universe, in the City of Gold, without change of cars
EXPRESS TRAIN
At All Hours.
Depot: Corner Faith and Repentance avenues.
All Cars First-Class.
Fare: Thy Sins.
NO HALF PASSES.
"He that believeth and is baptized shall be saved."—Bible.
PRINCE OF LIGHT,
President.

DAMNATION RAILROAD.
QUICK ROUTE TO HELL.
Many miles and much time saved by this line.
TERRIFIC SCENERY.
Through Dismal Swamp, Murderer's Gap, Hangman's Gorge, etc.; reach the Valley of the Shadow of Death at midnight, plunging its passengers into Eternal Woe.
Main Depot: Corner Unbelief and Disobedience streets.
☞Specials from Ingersoll Park, Dime Novel avenue, Theatre street, Blasphemers' hall, Smokers' furnace, Sample Room square.
Lightning train from Suicide avenue.
Extra train on Sunday. This train connects at Libertine landing with all night boats to Perdition.
Fare: Thy Soul.
"He that believeth not shall be damned."—Bible.
PRINCE OF DARKNESS,
President.

HIS FUNERAL TO-DAY.

His remains, accompanied by his brother, Mr. Ed. Willis, and brother-in-law, Mr. R. M. Adam, arrived in Augusta last night from Spartanburg, and were met by a large number of friends at the depot, whence they were taken to St. James church.

From 9:30 o'clock this morning the church will be open, and until the hour of the funeral the friends of the dead evangelist may have an opportunity to take a last look at his familiar features. The following gentlemen who have been selected to act his pall-bearers are requested to be at the church at 4:15 o'clock this afternoon.

From St. James church—Messrs. Eugene Foster, Josiah Miller and F. M. Stulb.

From St. John's church—Messrs. George Adam and W. M. Dunbar.

From Asbury church—Mr. J. E. Duren.

From St. Luke's church—Mr. W. O. Bohler.

From Broad Street church—Mr. J. H. Fearey.

All Methodist pastors and other minister in the city are invited to attend as honorary pall-bearers.

MEMORIAL SERVICES.

On next Sunday night, by request of the official board of St. James church, special memorial services will be held in honor of the late Rev. Miller Willis, in which the pastor and various lay members will take part.

MILLER WILLIS' BURIAL.

Beautiful Words by Rev. Mr. Yarbrough—The Throngs at the Memorial Services and at the Grave.

The memorial and funeral services over (and of) the remains of the late Miller Willis yesterday afternoon, at St. James' church, were impressive, imposing, touching.

St. James' is one of the largest churches in the South. Its commodious auditorium was filled with people.

A more thoroughly representative assembly of the people of Augusta could not be secured.

People of all classes, of all denominations, believers and non-believers, Hebrews and Gentiles, were there—for, than Miller Willis, there were but few better known men to the people of Augusta.

Ministers from a distance were present and many non-residents, lay admirers of the deceased were present at the services.

The tributes to the memory of the deceased were eloquent and from the heart. The funeral was one of the largest that has been seen in Augusta for years. In death, Miller Willis proved that he had many a friend in life.

THE EXERCISES.

The memorial exercises were begun at 4:30 o'clock by the reading of an appropriate hymn by Rev. Dr. Rees, pastor of the Methodist church of Watkinsville, Ga., which was followed by an earnest prayer by Rev.

W. C. Dunlap of Asbury church. This was followed by the reading of the 91st Psalm by Rev. B. E. L. Timmons of St. Luke's, and the reading of Scripture by Rev. W. W. Wadsworth of St. John's church, the 15th chapter of 1st Corinthians. The sermon by Rev. Mr. Yarbrough was a touching one. His eulogium of the deceased seemed inspired. There are few more powerful preachers than this eloquent gentleman. Seldom has he been more thoroughly imbued with interest in his subject than on yesterday afternoon. He knew Miller Willis and loved him. He spoke of the deceased as he thought of him. The result was a discourse of beautifully spoken words that touched all within sound of his voice.

His text was the last verse of the 15th chapter of 1st Corinthians. He stood, he said, in the presence of the mortal remains of a man who had given his whole life to the work of God; of saving souls; one who died leaving behind him only his Bible and his walking staff, showing that he had risen above the desire for money and had absolutely trampled worldly things under foot.

Some men, in making up an estimate of Miller Willis, had decided him a fanatic. There never was a greater mistake. The deceased was preëminently a man of practical common sense. If any doubted this, let him or her read the Bible which this saintly man had left behind him, and let him or her note the comments made therein by marginal notes.

If there were no hereafter; if Paganism were true; if

there were no heaven or hell, then Miller Willis had been a fool to consecrate himself to the service of God. But if there were, and that was demonstrated by the text and by the teachings of St. Paul, then Miller Willis was a profound philosopher.

The speaker said he had gone into his study to endeavor to prepare a sermon to preach over the remains of the deceased. But somebody had handed him Miller Willis' Bible. He read it and noticed the marginal comments and became absolutely lost, so far as any systematic preparation of a sermon was concerned. This Bible was his inspiration; that is, the man and his life as depicted in these comments gave him his text.

TO THE GRAVe.

After the sermon Rev. Mr. Frazier, of the Broad Street Methodist church, read, and the choir sang, "I would not live always," the congregation joining in the singing.

At the grave, the burial services were conducted by the pastor of Asbury church, assisted by the pastor of St. Luke.

After the grave was closed, the throng gathered about it and united in singing one stanza of "Sweet By-and-by."

The grave was lavishly covered with beautiful and appropriate floral offerings. Resting on a large pillow of elegant flowers was the inscription which was the watchword of the deceased during his life, "Have Faith in God."

CHAPTER XXIV.

ARTICLES FROM VARIOUS NEWSPAPERS, CHRISTIAN AND SECULAR, ON THE LIFE AND DEATH OF MILLER WILLIS.

BROTHER MILLER WILLIS.

A beautiful casket, containing the body of Brother Miller Willis, reached the depot in Augusta from Spartanburg, S. C., last Wednesday evening, was met by a number of ministers and laymen, and was carried by them to St. James' church to await the funeral service on the following afternoon.

Our city felt honored in having his precious remains entrusted to her, and with motherly tenderness and affection laid them away to rest until the resurrection morning. The casket was lowered into the grave amid the perfume of flowers, and the sobs and songs of many whom he had led to Christ and cheered on the way to Heaven.

That afternoon hour at his grave will not be forgotten soon. It was an hour of holy rapture of Christian triumph. After Brother Dunlap and Brother Timmons had read the service and pronounced the benediction, some one asked that the doxology, "Praise God from whom all blessings flow," be sung, and while the grave was being filled, other sweet songs were sung, and a number of Brother Willis' favorite exhortations were repeated. Having lived and labored like no other man, it was not surprising or inappropriate that he was buried like no other man.

We lingered there with overflowing hearts, and were sorry we had to leave. Personally, my heart received one of those dispensations of the Spirit "which passeth knowledge."

Like his Master, Brother Willis died poor. He was a follower of Him who was born in another man's manger, who was more homeless than the birds of the air, and the foxes that made their holes in the earth, while He lived, and was buried in another man's tomb when He died.

His Bible, and that long walking-staff on which his frail body leaned along his missions of love, were all he left. Next to keeping himself free from sin, it seemed to be his fixed purpose to let no money, beyond his strict necessities, stick to him.

His brother told me at his grave, that two gamblers in Charleston had told him to call on them whenever Miller Willis needed money. Many a pocket stood ready always to honor his draft. He could not be bribed; money could not do it; flattery could not do it; friendship could not do it. He knew no man "after the flesh." The best friend or benefactor he had on earth would hear his warnings, or feel his reproofs if they were needed.

Many said he was beside himself at times. Well, he was. But whenever he was beside himself, it was "unto God," and for this he had apostolic precedent. Others said he was a fanatic. I must give it as my belief, that Heaven could be easily organized on earth, and that the angels would be willing to come here and live, if all its inhabitants could take on the form of fanaticism that made radiant the life of our translated brother.

I spent the largest part of a day looking through his Bible. It had been rebound, and every other leaf was a blank that had been inserted by the binders, according to his directions, for notes, comments, and records of revivals and sermons, and different stages of personal experience. He took the Bible as a whole, and as he found it. Where human philosophy had mired down, Miller had shouted along on solid ground, possibly uttering a sigh as he passed its bones bleaching by the wayside. "Have faith in God," a favorite quotation, was woven into a beautiful wreath of flowers, and is now on his grave. Examine his Bible before you pronounce on the order of his mind.

He was lost in Christ.

I turned to the "Family Record" in his Bible. Here is all I found:

"S. M. Willis was born into the Kingdom of God 1864. He got Matt. xviii and 3d, in Augusta, Ga., and he knew it, and knows it now twenty-two years afterward. To God be all the glory!

"Was sanctified like I. Thess. 5th and 23d, Oct. 6th,

1877, while Brother Dunlap was preaching from Eph. 3d ch. and 16th to 21st verses.

"Now, O my Jesus, let me say, kept by the power of God, through faith until I get to Heaven, for Jesus' sake. Amen. Athens, Ga., July 11th, 1886.

"Read over 30 *Knows* in Epistle of John."

I expected more than this in this record; but, really it contains everything worth recording, and the thing that will outlive all other tests of a true life. This can lose nothing from the fires of the last day. It is the unfading and imperishable court-dress of Heaven, "Enoch walked with God." This was enough to justify the other part of the record, "and was not, for God took him."

He was a gallant soldier through the late war. I never heard him allude to it; saw no mention of it in his Bible. He seems to have had no existence until Christ found him and converted him, and from that time on his life was "hid with Christ in God." He came nearer doing all his talking in the language of the Bible than any man I ever saw. This was true before a congregation, and among his brethren and friends in social life, on meeting and in parting, on the streets and on the highways. He was a refined gentleman—neat in his dress, courteous in his demeanor, clean in his speech. Yes, yes. Who can recall an obscene expression or a vulgarism that ever polluted his lips since the dates of his conversion and sanctification? He professed sanctification. He records the time, the name of the preacher, the text; and let my tongue cleave to the roof of my mouth ere I seek to uproot that luminous mile-post planted by the Holy Ghost in this pilgrim's journey.

I came upon the words of the chief butler, in his Bible: "I remember my faults this day!" Right under it, Brother Willis asks, "Do I remember mine?" Then follow a number of dark spots that seemed to stand for what was on his mind. In Job I came upon the words, "I abhor myself, and repent in dust and ashes." Brother Willis writes right under it, "So do I."

In his correspondence he wrote, "Less than the least," before signing his name. Where is boasting then? It is excluded.

That Bible is a treasure. Happy he to whom it falls as an inheritance. It will be an heirloom among his brethren for generations to come. Many a pilgrim, bending in the direction he went, and straining his vision to catch the spires of the Eternal City, will be helped forward by the blazes cut by this man of God.

In Augusta his name is odorous, like a vase of fresh flowers. In Heaven his kinship to the Elder Brother and Saviour has been owned, and Brother Miller Willis is at home. GEO. W. YARBROUGH.

THE NAME OF MILLER WILLIS.

There is no name of any man, living or dead, spoken to-day in the city of Augusta so often as that of Miller Willis. His praise as a holy man is on the tongue of all who knew him, and he was universally known here, especially by the older citizens. He was born and brought up here. His funeral yesterday was the highest attestation to his worth as a religious man. He absolutely had nothing else to commend himself to the esteem of the people except his Christianity, for, as the preacher declared, he left nothing of this world's goods except his Bible and the staff he leaned upon when he walked. And yet, as the same preacher declared, returning from the cemetery, no other man could have called together such a thoroughly representative congregation by his death as attended the funeral of Miller Willis. There were representatives from every walk of life. The merchant, the lawyer, the mechanic, the every-day laborer, was largely represented. As has been announced, he fell on sleep at the home of his brother-in-law, Mr. Robt. M. Adam, in Spartanburg, S. C., on the morning of July 15th, 1891, about seven A. M. It was in perfect harmony with a life wholly given to God for the last twenty-five years that the last audible words sent back by him as his feet touched the Heavenly shore, "Trusting Jesus now and forever. Amen." And then, as if special favor was bestowed upon him to speak, even after life was gone out of the body, he called back to Brother Adam, "Do you hear? Trusting Jesus now and forever. Amen." Who that knew him can doubt for one moment that the first words that broke upon angelic ears was, "Trusting Jesus now and forever. Amen."

The funeral sermon was preached by Rev. George W.

Yarbrough, pastor of St. James, the church where he has had his membership, with only a short interval at one time, ever since he first joined the church. It was regarded by all as a very appropriate sermon, and the text, which was the last verse of the 15th chapter of 1st Corinthians, was powerfully enforced and illustrated by the life of Miller Willis. Brother Yarbrough said he had gone into his study in the morning to prepare a sermon, but some one had handed him Brother Willis' Bible the night before. He began reading the notes and comments, and soon became so absorbed that he forgot all about any effort to prepare a systematic sermon. He remarked to Brother Timmons and the writer on our way back from the grave that he had never spent such a day in his life, and that he felt like praising God at the top of his voice. As before remarked, the funeral was very largely attended. I heard one person remark that there were at least fifty carriages in the procession. Only think of the man who in life always signed himself to all his letters, "yours less than the least," with such a vast concourse of people following him to the grave. Surely it is in fulfillment even here on earth of the Divine word, "He that humbleth himself shall be exalted." This man of God, like his Divine Lord, first graduated in the lowest degree, and then went up to the highest. Some people during his life, that did not know him, had an idea that he professed to be an angel. Those of us that did know him, knew that he had the most abasing estimate of himself. I never knew any man who had a greater fear of the possibility of sinning. But his watchword at all times was, "Have Faith in God." It was fitting, therefore, that these words should stand out conspicuously over the head of his grave: "Have Faith in God." But how shall we draw the true picture of this holy man. He was the soul of honor. He was a very Chesterfield in his politeness toward women. And while he never let an opportunity escape him to speak to them about their souls, he always raised his hat while he did it. I have had him in my house for weeks, and while he enjoyed the freedom of a member of my own family he never forgot his native and Christian politeness. I could write a whole volume of incidents showing that he was a man of one thought and work.

Brother Yarbrough in looking through his Bible was particularly struck with the fact that, while it is full of facts and incidents (it is interleaved with blank leaves) there is not one item about himself or any one else except of a purely religious nature. On the blank leaf for family records this is the entry, "S. M. Willis was born into the kingdom of God, 1864; he got Matthew xviii: 3, in Augusta, Ga.—was converted, and he knew it, and he knows it now twenty-two years afterwards. To God be all the glory. Was sanctified like I. Thes. v:23, October 6th, 1877, while Brother W. C. Dunlap was preaching from Eph. iii:14–21. Now oh, my Jesus let me say, kept by the power of God through faith, until I get to heaven, for Jesus' sake. Amen.

I failed to say in the right place, that all the pastors

(Methodist) of the city—including Dr. Rees, of Watkinsville, participated in the funeral services in some way.

Shall we ever see his like again? A prominent Presbyterian said to me to-day, "He was the best man I ever knew;" said he, "Many ministers will die and be forgotten, but his name and influence will live on for good to souls forever.

I feel for one, that there is a new tie to draw me on to heaven, and I expect, by grace, to meet him there.— *W. C. Dunlap, in Way of Life.*

CHAPTER XXV.

MILLER WILLIS.

Way of Life.

Let me write a few words about my old *spiritual father*. The name of Miller Willis will always have a warm place in my heart. It's beyond my comprehension to fathom the love that I possessed in my heart for him. When Brother Adam told me that Miller was gone, my heart cried out: "Farewell, thou man of God, thou art gone, but not forgotten." "Blessed are the dead who die in the Lord." No man need to write his past biography to let the world know his worth; his works will follow him.

I remember when I was eight years old, one night he and Brother Dunlap took tea at a neighbor's house. I went over to see him, and O, well do I remember his taking me up in his lap, laying his hand on my head, saying, "One of these days little Jimmie will preach the Gospel." I have never forgotten those words. Ten years had passed by; I had not seen Miller in that time and he had never seen me. Two years ago while conducting a religious meeting in Athens, Ga., with a certain religious movement, one night I heard a man hollow out while I was reading the Bible, "Praise the Lord." I knew it was Miller Willis. While I continued reading, Miller jumped up and shouted out: "Glory to God, there is my little Jimmie preaching the Gospel, whom I have not seen before in ten years, but I knew the Lord would answer my prayer."

To-day I am pastor of one of the Baptist churches and Missionary of the Fairfield Association. I know to-day that this is all a fulfillment of Miller Willis' prophecy. "Trusting Jesus, that is all," were his last words, and then passed into eternity the grandest man in the history of the Methodist Church. As I read an account of his funeral, I was lead to inquire, "was this man the son of an emperor, of the king that wore the crown?" He was not, my friends. But he is now enjoying the immortality of the soul, and is a heavenly prince in the glory world. The grave holds all that is left of him, the grand, noble, well pleased servant of God. Now that soul that loved, that mind that taught and has impressed itself upon the world, must come back, for if thoughts live, will that precious thought cease? "*In reason he speaks and in example he lives.*" Such was said of Garfield and can be said of Miller Willis. His thoughts and mighty deeds still flourish in structure. There was a man in Bible history that killed more in his death than in life, and I believe that to be true with Miller Willis. Our loss is his gain. The sufferings of his life were as fruitful of blessings as the toils; Christ was all his theme. He has been, from my first acquaintance with him, an uncommonly spiritual Christian, exhibiting the richest graces of a Godly life. Every subject on which he conversed, every book he read, had a tendency to suggest some peculiarly spiritual train of thought till it seemed to me, as I have said, Christ was all his theme. If he was a crank he has gone to the great asylum above where there is a good keeper. He was a man no doubt, who had sorrows at times, but his joys outnumbered his sorrows. He is gone! It is all as God would have it, and our duty is but to bend meekly to His will, and wait, in faith and in patience, till we also shall be summoned home. Life's race well run, life's work well done, life's crown well won. Now comes rest. May a double portion of his heavenly spirit fall upon us.

JAS. W. KRAMER,
Pastor Red Bank Baptist Church,
Columbia, S. C.

RECOLLECTIONS OF MILLER WILLIS.

Way of Life.

I am truly glad that the Rev. W. C. Dunlap has "taken in hand to draw up a narrative" (Luke i: 1, New Version) of the ways and works of that earnest and devout man of God, the late Miller Willis. I knew Brother Willis quite well, when I was editor of the *Southern Christian Advocate* in Charleston, S. C., from 1878 to 1886. He was living at that time in Charleston, and we frequently met in the services of Trinity Church and elsewhere. I never heard him say a word on any other subject than religion; and it was generally his personal experience of religion. He was beyond any man I have ever known, "a man of one book"—*homo unius libri*, as Mr. Wesley pedantically calls it. And he was just as distinctly "a man of one work"—THIS ONE THING I DO.—(Phil. iii : 13).

There is an old Latin proverb, "I will find a way or make one." So it was with dear Miller. If an opportunity occurred to work for the Master he would use it. If no opportunity occurred, he would make one. He was instant in season and *out of season*. (Italics mine).

He was one of my best friends. Of this he gave me palpable evidence now and again. Let me give an instance. I was spending the summer with my family on Sullivan's Island. I was pastor of a Union church over there and would sometimes exchange pulpits with the city clergy. I had preached one Sunday morning at the First Baptist Church and was hurrying to catch the Island boat (1 P. M.) I met Miller near the market. "How d'ye do? How d'ye do? Excuse me, I'm in a hurry, I want to catch the boat." "Let the boat alone, and remember the Sabbath day to keep it holy!" thundered out my friend, who wouldn't suffer what he considered a sin in his brother, without a faithful and manly rebuke. SAMUEL A. WEBER.

Aiken, S. C.

S. MILLER WILLIS.

I am glad to hear that we are to have a biography of Brother S. Miller Willis. If anything of the man can be transferred to the book—if it can be made to breathe out the meek, gentle, trustful, faithful spirit which filled him, and in which he lived, moved and had his being every moment of his active, earnest, happy life, after he received the baptism of fire, it will doubtless do much good.

He came to my charge, King's Ferry and Hilliard, during the fall of 1889, in company with Brother R. O. Smith, to assist me in revival services. I felt the force of his pure, consecrated life when first we met. He seemed to me like a fully equipped warrior fairly panting for the conflict with sin, and from his first arrival until the day of his departure, during several eventful weeks, in high places and in low places, and among the most hardened roughs of those milling towns, he waged a constant, untiring and unflinching warfare. His sincerity could not be doubted by the most skeptical. This, together with his great humility and sweetness of spirit, was his protection among the most abandoned characters. His faith was Jacob-like—as a prince he prevailed with God in prayer, more especially in private prayer, and thus honoring God in secret, he was rewarded openly with indomitable energy and courage, and with power to prevail with the most hardened sinners. He sowed down both communities with the most pungent tracts, varied and judiciously presented, to suit the conditions of those with whom he labored.

His pointed questions put to those with whom he met, often produced the deepest convictions for sin and neglect of duty. His most usual question on meeting a stranger was not if he or she were members of a church, but if they were regenerated or born of the spirit, or had passed from death unto life.

While with us, he went into one house, the occupant of which was a member of a church, and asked the privilege of praying with them, and was refused, with the statement that they did not have the time; but instead of being discouraged he proceeded to administer a telling rebuke. Oh! if we had more saints who could and would rebuke sin, in high and low, rich and poor, regardless of relationships, in the spirit of meekness, wickedness would then lose its respectability.

He had no use for superficial work in revivals, but urged penitents to seek until they received a clear consciousness of salvation, through the witness of God's Spirit with their spirits that they were His children.

He ran down to Jacksonville on the morning train while with us, and spent the day in visiting the haunts of wickedness, and especially the whiskey saloons, and distributed tracts, and warned them of the judgment to come. He remarked on returning to us from his disagreeable day's work, that Jacksonville, Florida, was a much better place in his estimation than Charleston, S.

C., for he said if he had done the same thing in the latter place, he would have received several cursings.

Brother A. O. MacDonell, General Passenger Agent of the F. C. & P. Railroad system, our Methodist railroad prince and friend of Methodist preachers, at my request, kindly sent Brother Willis a half fare permit over all branches of their system, and then the dear, sweet-spirited saint bid us an affectionate farewell, and started southward to labor in Manatu village on the Manatu river, where, from all accounts, he made a lasting impression, and had many conversions and sanctifications as seeds to his labors.

From this place I think he returned homeward to appear no more among us. I consider it one of the greatest privileges of my life to have met him and to have been associated with him even for a short while, in our Lord's delightful employ.

Heaven is sweeter in anticipation by the emigration thither of dear Brother Miller Willis, for he is only gone before to await the oncoming of the vast host with, and for whom he labored.

"Servant of God, well done,
Rest from thy loved employ."

Your Brother, ROBERT M. EVANS.
Key Largo, Fla.

From Way of Life.

THE TEXT AND SERMON UNDER WHICH MILLER WILLIS WAS WHOLLY SANCTIFIED.

BY REV. W. C. DUNLAP.

Ephesians iii : 14-21.

"For this cause I bow my knees unto the Father of our Lord Jesus Christ, of whom the whole family in heaven and earth is named, that He would grant you, according to the riches of His glory, to be strengthened with might by His Spirit in the inner man. That Christ may dwell in your hearts by faith; that ye being rooted and grounded in love, may be able to comprehend with all saints what is the breadth, and length, and depth, and height; and to know the love of Christ, which passeth knowledge, that ye might be filled with all the fullness of God. Now, unto Him that is able to do exceeding abundantly above all that we ask or think, according to the power that worketh in us, unto Him be glory in the church by Christ Jesus throughout all ages, world without end. Amen."

The fifteenth verse is a parenthesis. Why? Because the passage makes perfect sense without it—read it over and see.

Paul was in prison. This is more than a prayer "that ye (they) faint not at my (his) tribulations for you, (them) which is your (their) glory." Thirteenth verse. If they get what this prayer includes, they will not only get where they will not "faint" at his tribulations," but also their own. In short, this is a prayer embracing all the successional steps leading up to and culminating in their entire sanctification. The greater includes the lesser. To get them wholly sanctified was the divine way to head off spiritual "fainting." As it was then, so it is now. Can we follow Paul in this wonderful prayer? Only by the Spirit's help. We have a succession of climaxes, all so interblended as to make a perfect chain. They mark by gradation the steps of a child of God from conversion to entire sanctification. "For this cause I bow my knees unto the Father of our Lord Jesus Christ, that He would grant you to be strengthened—strengthened in the inner man—with might in the inner man—strengthened with *might* by His Spirit in the inner man—that he would grant you to be strengthened with *might* by His Spirit in the inner man according to his glory—according to the *riches* of His glory."

All this to one end: "That Christ may dwell in your hearts by faith." This also to a single end: "That ye being rooted and grounded in love;" and this for a single purpose: "May be able to comprehend with all saints what is the breadth, and length, and depth, and height." Further: "And to know the love of Christ that passeth knowledge." And all this to one great consummation: "That ye might be *filled* with *all* the *fullness* of God." Then as if in offering the prayer for others he had reached the glorious acme of divine "fullness" himself, he breaks out in one of those grandly inspired doxologies. "Now unto Him that is *able* to do for us *all* that we ask; now unto Him that is *able* to do for us *above* all that we ask; now unto Him that is *able* to do for us *abundantly* above *all* that we ask; now unto Him that is able to do *exceeding abundantly above all* that we ask *or think*, according to the *power* that worketh in us. To Him be glory in the church throughout all ages, world without end. Amen."

When the preacher got to the twentieth verse, Miller Willis was seen suddenly to drop on his knees, but as this was nothing unusual, it was not thought strange of, until directly he rose to his feet exclaiming at the top of his voice, "I've got it; I've got it!" "Got what? Brother Miller," asked the preacher. "Got what I lost down at the Richmond camp-meeting," he replied. "And what's that?" again asked the preacher. "I've got sanctification, glory to God! and I defy men or devils to take it away from me this time." In telling his experience afterwards he said, "I first felt if God could do all that Paul said He could do in the twentieth verse, then He was certainly able to sanctify a little fellow like me." It is proper to remark that he had obtained the experience a few weeks before under the preaching of the sainted B. F. Farris; but Brother Farris began to put questions to him which, as he said, caused him to take his eyes off of Jesus, and lo! when he looked for the blessing it was gone. From then until he re-obtained the experience he was indeed almost like a crazy man.

Oh, that God would so wake up all who once had but have since lost the experience, that, like Miller Willis, hey'd never stop until they got it back.

CHAPTER XXVI.

His Last Days.

I need not enlarge on the incidents of his going up to his Heavenly home, since this has been done by an eye witness of his departure. A triumphant close of such a life as he lived was the natural expectation of all who knew him. He himself, while living, delighted to refer and dwell upon such scenes. He gave great emphasis to Mr. Wesley's testimony to the early Methodists: "Our people die well." One instance I have heard him often mention. A brother Lawrence up North; he was a bright light in the experience of entire sanctification, but he fell a victim to consumption early in life. He was a pastor in the M. E. Church, and greatly beloved by his people. They clung to him with the tenacity of an undying love; but the end came. With a number of his congregation gathered around him, he said, "Raise me up." They raised him up in his bed. With a heavenly glow upon his face, the dying minister raised his hand and eye upward and said, "Go tell them! Go *tell* them! I'm going up with the *great* procession, and to meet me there"—he was gone. With what a thrill upon his hearers have I heard him describe this victorious death. They never met on earth, but they are together in glory.

We are on a question of no minor importance. There

is danger in the oft-repeated remark of these days: "Show me how a man lived, and its a matter of no consequence how he dies." If we live right we shall die right; all are agreed on that. But dying testimony is of vital importance to the world. Jesus Himself left His dying testimony: "Father forgive them; they know not what they do. Father into thy hands I commend my spirit." The Devil has brought the Christ-like profession of medicine under contribution to his satanic uses, as he will every blessing, if he can, so that dying people are drugged now into a state of insensibility. He has two purposes in this. First, he does not want the testimony of God's saints as they leave the world. Second, he is afraid to risk the honest confession of his own servants. It is a significant fact that when Miller Willis came to his last moments he rejected all earthly palliatives or stimulants. He died in the *unclouded* light of the Son of Righteousness. His excessive labors; his constant fastings, and, in some senses, his *cause* of all the churches (oh, how he loved the church of God, and that branch especially to which he belonged) gradually but surely sapped the foundation of his not very robust constitution. Hemorrhage supervened; not frequent at first, but violent enough to alarm his friends. Strong efforts were made to slow him down in his work, but this was only temporary relief; besides the very brethren who were so solicitous for his life, were ofttimes the ones who most delighted to have him as their helper; and there was this feeling: "Well, Miller Willis belongs to God and He will take care of him." True, but God's normal method of taking care of people physically, as well as spiritually, is according to His laws. Brother Willis was not a stalwart in his physical man. He was of delicate mould. Very few men would have lasted as long as he did, making the same time in every-thing they undertook. "The King's business requireth haste," was the principle upon which he acted. As he was a man of "one book," so he was, for the last twenty years of his life, a man of one work. No itinerant Methodist preacher is more constantly engaged in the Master's work than was he. He spent two winters in Florida, ostensibly for his health, but even there he was in labors more abundant. He was there when he saw the end was near. He returned to his beloved Augusta, from where, after resting a week or so at the house of his very dear friends, Brother and Sister Josiah Miller, he went on to the home of his darling sister, Mrs. Robert M. Adam, Spartanburg, S. C., where he breathed his last.

Sam Jones once remarked, in preaching before the North Georgia Conference, that he would like to preach the funeral of some preacher who killed himself working for God and souls; he thought the angels would compose his congregation. This man was not a preacher after man's estimate or authority, but in the divinest sense he was a New Testament preacher. I believe Miller Willis gave his life for the salvation of souls. He died a martyr as truly as any of those who went to the stake.

Do not misunderstand me. He never spared himself so long as he was able to go. He fasted oftener and longer than any man I ever knew. He prayed more than once all night long. I have known him to work until he literally dropped in his tracks. He had a way of kneeling that indicated the man's humility. He never knelt except with his face in his hands, and his hands on the floor or ground. I have seen him in such agony of soul that great drops of sweat would break out all over his face, and no doubt from his whole body. I have actually trembled with apprehension for the result to his lungs. I may be mistaken, but I verily believe his hemorrhages were brought on in this way. I looked for them long before they came. His first hemorrhage that I knew of took place in Gainesville, (Ga.

During the first few years of my acquaintance with him he was an intense sufferer from his spine, reaching up into the back of his head. He also suffered greatly at times with neuralgia. A very painful and even ludicrous incident occurred once in my attempt to "treat him" for spinal trouble. I say ludicrous, for, although it involved great suffering, I could not help laughing after Miller got better. In my ignorance I actually saturated the poor fellow's neck and back part of his head with croton oil. The result was a blister nearly six inches long, that made a sore for days, so that he could not turn his head. They say "what won't kill will cure," and I do believe it did him great good, for I never heard him complain like he did before.

His hemorrhages become more and more frequent, until at length it became evident to his brethren he could not hold up much longer, unless they could be stopped. One thing that has always made me believe his hemorrhages were the result of excessive labor, and not from consumption of the ordinary sort, was because he never had any bad cough or expectorated as a consumptive does. His friends did all in their power to stop him, but, like his Divine Lord, the zeal of his Lord's house had eaten him up.

The way opened for him to go down into South Georgia, and then on in to Florida. As he went he was instant in season and out of season, always abounding in the work of the Lord. He was thrown with Rev. R. O. Smith, a local preacher and evangelist; in him he found a true fellow-worker. Together they labored for at least two winters in Florida. God wonderfully blessed their labors in converting sinners and in sanctifying believers. Brother Willis had many homes; this fact we have alluded to in another connection. We mention it here only to say that the words of our Divine Lord were literally fulfilled in his case—he forsook houses and lands and all else besides of an earthly character, and in return he had fathers and mothers and brothers and sisters in abundance, with persecutions. Among the "homes," he had, none were more lovingly tendered him, nor was he more joyfully welcomed or tenderly cared for than at

Brother —— Lott's, in South Georgia. Being a man blessed with means, and himself and wife wholly consecrated to God, Miller never lacked for "any good thing," if these loving friends could reach him.

The time was at hand for him to exchange an earthly for the heavenly home. These kind friends, with many others, would have had him stay down here if they could—not in opposition to, but in harmony with, the Father's will.

The writer, together with many others, called on him for the last time as he passed through Augusta. Never can I forget the room where we knelt and prayed together at Brother Joe Miller's, or the "Good-bye," and the old time embrace, and the whispered—on account of weakness—"God bless you—we'll meet up yonder." The next time I saw him he was "asleep in Jesus," not dead, oh no, for "death hath no more dominion over him," he is only asleep. Lying there in that beautiful casket, it looked like he ought to open his eyes, or, more natural and like in life, cry out to those who gathered about him for a last look, "Who's converted?" and "Who knows if they were to drop dead this moment they'd go straight to heaven?"

And thus ends our story, imperfectly told; alas, no one is so conscious of it as he who has tried to tell it. But we lay it upon the altar on which Miller Willis rested his all for both worlds, even upon Him who said "the altar sanctifieth the gift," and our prayer and faith

LIFE OF S. MILLER WILLIS.   293

is, that He will continue to bless, through this affectionate and sincere, though humble effort, the life and labors of our sainted and glorified Miller Willis. "Amen, and Hallelujah!"

FINIS.